Desmond

The Lifegiving Word
A Prayer Book

the columba press

First published in 2008 by
the columba press
55A Spruce Avenue, Stillorgan Industrial Park,
Blackrock, Co Dublin

Designed by Bill Bolger
Cover photograph by courtesy of *Integritas*
Origination by The Columba Press
Printed in Ireland by ColourBooks Ltd, Dublin

ISBN 978-1-85607-617-3

Acknowledgements

Four books to which I made constant reference must be named. *The Theological Dictionary of the New Testament* by Geoffrey by W. Bromley (Eerdmans), *Expository Dictionary of Bible Word* by Laurence O. Richards (Regency), *The New SCM Dictionary of Christian Spirituality*, Ed. Philip Sheldrake (SCM Press), *Character Strengths and Virtues* by C. P. Peterson and E. P. Seligman (Oxford University Press) have all contributed to the final presentation of this book. I have used lecture notes from Jerome Murphy O'Connor OP, Dr Tom Rosica and Professor John Bailey in Jerusalem.

I wish to express my deep thanks to my Oblate community for their constant encouragement. I thank Sister Ethna Leonard and her Mercy community who improved the text in so many ways and I thank of my cousins Evin and Rena whose sensitive suggestions have enhanced the presentation..

Seán O Boyle, of The Columba Press has been enthusiastic and helpful from the beginning.

I have used the New Revised Standard Version of the New Testament.

Contents

Special Times

God's Word

The Hebrew word *dabhar* is used to describe God's word in the Old Testament. *Dahbar* means much more than a sound in our ear or a thought in our head. It is the word which made the world. It is a creative word, a word-event. God's word never leaves the believing listener the same. When a word from God is received with an open heart, that person is enriched and gently changed.

Two thousand years ago, God spoke his deepest Word to us – Jesus. The humanity of Jesus was the full manifestation of all that God is. And every word spoken by Jesus was God's word too.

For this reason the New Testament still speaks God's word to us. St Paul told Timothy that the words of scripture instruct us, correct any evil among us, teach us how to be holy and equip us for every good work. Every word in scripture is God saying 'I love you' in many different ways. God cannot speak any other word, because God is love.

Jesus told us that God's word is like a seed; it initiates life within us. St Peter tells us that we can be 'born anew … through the living and enduring word of God'. Paul said to the Colossians, 'Let the word of Christ dwell in you richly.' Each word in scripture can transform us because God's word is God himself.

Constantly recall that God's word is always new each time you read it.

Listening with the heart to God's Word

We listen to words at many levels. Some words go no further than our ears. Some enter our minds and make us think. Other words touch our surface feelings with shallow joy or momentary sadness.

The deepest form of listening takes place when we listen with the ears of the heart. The words then affect us profoundly; they change us. This is real listening. We usually listen in this way to close friends because the words come to us wrapped in love. These words enhance our sense of self-worth and change the way we look at the world.

This is how God wants us to hear the word in scripture. Jesus told Martha that Mary had chosen a better way because, rather than serving his meal or speaking to him, she sat with him and listened. Recall also that on the Road to Emmaus, the two disciples' hearts were on fire while listening to god's word: 'Were not our hearts burning within us while he was talking to us on the road, while he was openin g the scriptures to us?"

Having listened to the word, your deep feeling may be one of love, joy, peace or freedom, one of need, of hope or of confidence, one of awe or wonder, one of being called with a desire to respond or a feeling of regret for the past. Whatever your feeling is, it is your prayer from your heart.

Note: If, on reading God's word, you have feelings of fear, of constant guilt or of excessive anxiety, it is advisable to speak to a friend or to a spiritual guide about it.

Using this Book

These are not prayers to be said; they are words to be listened to.

In order to make your prayerful listening more personal, I offer, in heart-to-heart direct speech, what I believe the New Testament is saying to you. The Good News is always addressed to you personally. After each quote, I give the reference to its source so that you may read it in the original when you wish. The explanations of the themes may help you from time to time.

The sessions are set out in the form of three for each day. Don't be put off by this. You may use them for daily prayer or choose a subject from the alphabetical index which suits you at a particular time. During liturgical seasons such as Easter or Christmas you may like to choose the prayer-themes indicated.

As you read the word, it may help to close your eyes and wait for the deep feeling to come. This feeling comes from God's Spirit in your spirit, so that the prayer becomes uniquely yours.

Before prayer it will help to breathe deeply and slowly a few times, while trusting that God is going to speak to you. You may find your favourite picture or icon helpful.

If one of the scripture words from your prayer-time helps

you deeply, you could recall it when you work around the house, take a walk, drive, sit in a bus or play golf.

Finally, imagine if you met Jesus and he called you by name, saying, 'I have some good news for you.' Ask yourself how you would react. Would you speak or would you listen deeply?

Let the word of Christ in all its richness have a home in you.
(Colossians 3:16)

You may find this prayer useful to begin your time with the word.

> *May you, the God of our Lord Jesus Christ,*
> *give me a spirit of wisdom*
> *and perception of what you reveal,*
> *bringing me to full knowledge of yourself,*
> *as I listen to your words.*

(cf Col 1:9-10)

WEEK ONE

In the Sacred Books,
the Father who is in heaven
meets his children with great love and speaks to them.
The force and the power of the word of God is so great
that it stands as
– a support and energy for the church
– the strength of faith for her children
– the food of the soul and
– the pure and perennial source of the spiritual life.

Vatican Council II, *Word of God*, 21.

God is a community of three persons in a relationship of infinite love. We are privileged to have a loving relationship with each member of that divine community. The love of the Father for his Son is much more than a source of inspiration for us. We actually share in it because he loves each of us with that same unconditional love. St John's gospel tells us that 'God so loved the world that he gave his only Son'.

To be a Christian then is not only to imitate Jesus or to obey the commandments. In isolation, this obedience would reduce our Christian lives to mere morality. Authentic faith leads us beyond these limits into the richness of a divine relationship. We are called, not only to imitate Jesus but to have a privileged identity with him.

In our baptism Jesus has already given us a share in the glory that was his before the world began. This gift enables us to share the interpersonal life of the Trinity. Jesus' prayer to the Father during his Last Supper was, 'As you Father are in me and I am in you, may they also be in us.' We were baptised into the love of the Trinity in the name of the Father, the Son and the Holy Spirit. By the power of the Holy Spirit we are identified with the Son in his being loved by the Father. We are immersed in the triune love within God.

Theologian Tina Beattie puts it this way: 'We are baptised, incorporated into the Trinitarian love of God through the maternal body of the Church.'

Now prayerfully contemplate the love of the Father for his Son, into which you were baptised and in which you are called to live and to grow.

God is Love

In the beginning, my Son was with me in love. With him I shared the Godhead from all eternity.   *ref: Jn 1:1*

I loved him before the foundation of the world.   *ref: Jn17:23, 34*

I continue to lovingly glorify my Son with the glory he had in my presence before the world existed.   *ref: Jn 17:1, 2*

He is the reflection of my glory and the exact imprint of my very being, always close to my heart. *ref: Heb 1:3 and Jn 1:18*

When you see him, you see me, because he is in me and I am in him.   *ref: Jn 14:9-10*

I love my Son and show him all that I am doing and my Son does only what he sees me doing.   *ref: Jn 5:19*

The glory I gave to him, he has now given to you, so that you may be one in love with us and with all believers.   *ref: Jn 17:22*

I filled him with the joy of the Holy Spirit, and his joy is now yours.   *ref: Jn 15:11*

My Son could not describe his love for you better than to say that he loved you as I love him.   *ref: Jn 15:9*

Some Christians find the Holy Trinity an abstract doctrine and not very relevant to their lives. They consider it a mystery in the sense of being something impossible to understand, rather than an invitation to endless love and understanding. The fact that God is three persons in one, is a mystery so profoundly deep that it is endlessly rich. In this sense St Paul speaks of 'the mystery of God'. Without this insight, our life journey could be little more than a moral effort to live by law alone.

This journey begins as we seek to understand and appreciate the words of Jesus at his final meal: 'The world must recognise that I love the Father.' Only then will we appreciate that we are baptised into this movement of divine love, and that our Christian lives are a journey into believing it more fully every day. We have the privilege of participating in the intimate love-life of God through the power of the Holy Spirit who pours God's love into our hearts.

All authentic Christian spirituality is intimately connected with the Trinity. We are called to accept, to nurture and to radiate to others the love of the Son for the Father. This love is within us through the power of the Holy Spirit.

God sent the Spirit into our hearts enabling us to say with him, 'Abba, Father.' When we come closer to what that means, then our Christian life is not a lonely moral effort but an ever increasing participation in the love of Jesus for his Father.

Now gratefully contemplate this love, in which you are privileged to participate.

God is Love

As I came into the world, my words were, 'See, God, I have come to do your will'.   *ref: Heb 10:5-7*

I did nothing on my own, but only what I saw my Father doing.   *ref: Jn 5:19*

My teaching was not mine, but his who sent me. I was always seeking the glory of my Father.   *ref: Jn 7:16-18*

Knowing that my Father's word is eternal life, I spoke just as the Father told me.   *ref: Jn 12:50*

At my Last Supper I looked towards heaven and I prayed, 'Father, the hour has come; glorify your Son so that the Son may glorify you.'   *ref: Jn 17:14*

As I left the supper room, my words were, 'The world must recognise that I love the Father and do as he commanded me. Rise, let us be on our way.'   *ref: Jn 14:31*

I was glorified in my death because my Father was glorified in me.   *ref: J.13:31, 32*

I came from the Father and entered the world. Again I left the world and went to the Father.   *ref: Jn 16:28*

Now he has sent my Spirit into your heart, so that you can join me in lovingly saying 'Abba, Father.'   *ref: Gal: 4:6*

In the end I will hand over the kingdom to my Father, so that he can be all in all.   *ref: 1 Cor 15:24-26*

For the pagans, prayer could be described as raising their hearts and minds to their gods, but Christian prayer cannot be adequately described as raising one's heart and mind to God. Rather it is the privilege of stepping into the movement of love between the divine persons in the Trinity. It is the supreme privilege of identifying with the Word in his active love of his Father.

In the first chapter of his gospel John writes: 'In the beginning was the Word, and the Word was with God.' The words 'with God' are an attempt to translate the Greek words *pros ton theon* which literally express a *motion towards*. It is difficult to translate this phrase exactly into English.

The word *pros* means 'movement towards'. *Theos* means God. In telling us that the Word was 'towards' God, we get a hint about an active movement of love between the Word and the Father from all eternity. With great care, we might call this prayer-in-God – this flow of love which has been taking place from the Word towards the Father before the world was made.

In our prayer we are gifted to join in this movement of love between the Son and the Father. In prayer we are graced to join with the Spirit of Jesus living in us saying 'Abba, Father.' This is how Paul speaks of it to the Galatians: 'God sent the Spirit of his Son into our hearts, crying Abba, Father'.

In the first centuries, Christians said this prayer: 'Glory be to the Father, through the Son, in the Holy Spirit.' This is the heart of Christian prayer.

Now meditate deeply on your privileged participation in this beautiful movement within the Trinity.

God is Love

Through my Son and in his one Spirit, you have prayerful access to me, God your Father.   *ref: Eph 2:18*

I invite you to join the Spirit of my Son in praying 'Abba, Father' from your heart.   *ref: Gal 4:6*

It is a privilege to join him when you pray. He is always interceding for you according to my mind.   *ref: Rom 8:26, 27*

The Spirit teaches and interprets spiritual things to you who are spiritual.   *ref: 1 Cor 2:10-13*

Only my Spirit whom you have received comprehends what is truly mine, so that when you pray you may understand the gifts I bestow on you.   *ref: 1 Cor 2:11-12*

My Holy Spirit is the Spirit of truth. He will guide you into all truth for he speaks whatever he hears.   *ref: Jn 16:13*

You pray best when, like Mary at Bethany, you sit and listen to the words of my Son.   *ref: Lk 10:39*

Be filled with my Spirit as you pray, singing psalms and hymns and spiritual songs to me in your heart, giving me thanks at all times for everything in the name of my Son Jesus Christ.   *ref: Eph 5:18-20*

The Greek word for mystery – *musterion* – occurs twenty seven times in the New Testament, twenty of them in the writings of Paul. A mystery in the New Testament is something so deep that it is endlessly rich. Our only approach to a Christian mystery is to accept our inability to fully comprehend the richness and depth of its beauty.

In his first letters to the Corinthians and to Timothy and in Colossians, Paul speaks about 'the mystery of God', 'the mystery of Christ', 'the mystery of the faith' and 'the mystery of God's message'.

In his letter to the Colossians he says that he wants our hearts to be encouraged and united in love so that we may have all the riches of assured understanding and 'knowledge of God's mystery which is Christ himself'. He tells them that God has at last made known to all, 'the riches of the glory of this mystery which is Christ in you, your hope of glory'. In second Corinthians this mystery is, 'The light of the gospel of the glory of Christ who is the image of God'.

Paul says that he has the responsibility 'to make the word of God fully known, the mystery that has been hidden throughout the ages'. We too are servants and privileged ministers of that mystery, but it is only by revelation and prayer that we can receive and grow in it.

Now contemplate God speaking to you about the mystery of Christ in your life.

The Mystery of Christ

I, the God who created all things wish you to know the plan of a mystery hidden for ages in my heart.   *ref: Eph 3:9*

Be strengthened through the proclamation of my Son who is the mystery kept hidden for long ages, and which now invites you to the obedience of faith.   *ref: Rom 16:25-27*

I want your heart to be encouraged and united with others in love, so that you may have all the riches and understanding of the mystery of my Son.   *ref: Col 2:2*

In him all the treasures of wisdom and knowledge are hidden.   *ref: Col 2:3*

I want to encourage your heart with all the riches of this great mystery – the boundless riches of Christ.   *ref: Col 2:3 and Eph 3:8*

I want to strengthen you according to my gospel through the revelation of this great mystery.   *ref: Rom 16:25*

You are a servant of this mystery that has been hidden for ages, the mystery which is Christ in you, your hope of glory.   *ref: Col 1:25-27*

I want you to pray with thanksgiving that doors will be opened for the declaration of this mystery everywhere and for its clear revelation in your own heart.   *ref: Col 4:2-4*

The People of God in the Old Testament were like us in their desire to see God. In the book of Exodus, God forbade the making of all images, not because God is remote, but because no words, no concepts, no images and no power of imagination can define or describe God. Images of God could give the impression of comprehending the incomprehensible and of limiting the limitless. Israel was never permitted to see God's form as when God spoke from the fire or from the cloud.

However, in the opening word of Hebrews we read: 'Long ago God spoke to our ancestors in many and various ways by the prophets, but in these last days he has spoken to us by a Son … He is the reflection of God's glory and the exact imprint of God's very being.'

Paul makes this great truth even clearer to the Colossians: 'He is the image of the invisible God, the firstborn of all creation; for in him all things in heaven and on earth were created … For in him all the fullness of God was pleased to dwell.'

At the Last Supper, Jesus made this great revelation to Philip: 'Whoever has seen me has seen the Father.' Jesus is not the Father but the one sent by the Father. The message he gives by his life is the story of God. His voice is the voice of God. He is the human image of God.

Now prayerfully contemplate the spoken words of him who is God's greatest Word to you.

The Image of God

No one has ever seen God. I, who am close to his heart have made him known to you.   *ref: Jn 1:18*

I am the image of the invisible God, the firstborn of all creation.   *ref: Col 1:15*

In me you see his glory – the glory of the Father's only Son. *ref: Jn 1:14*

I have come from above. I speak the words of God. I testify to what I have seen and heard.   *ref: Jn 3:31-34*

If you know me, you will know my Father also. Now you can know him and you have seen him.   *ref: Jn 14:7*

My Father sent me into the world, so that you might have life through me.   *ref: 1 Jn 4:9*

I am the way, and the truth and the life. No one comes to the Father except through me.   *ref: Jn 14:6*

Whoever has seen me has seen the Father because I am in the Father and the Father is in me.   *ref: Jn 14:9-11*

The Father has now predestined you to be my image, so that I may be the firstborn of his earthly family.   *ref: Rom 8:29*

We live with a constant avalanche of words into our ears. Mobile phones, radio, television screens and the Internet invade our minds. We know that many of the words we read or hear are just spam.

Not all words are of equal value. Some words are words of care, concern, support and love. These enrich us. Some messages we receive are reliable and beneficial to us. Sometimes they are not. Often they are basically manipulative or seductive, just subtle efforts to have us part with our money or to win our votes.

God's words are different. They are always words for our good, like the words of a true friend. They express God's desire for our welfare and they give us guidance and energy so that we can become our best human selves and God-like.

In the Semite world, the one sent is the presence of the one who sends. The presence of Jesus is the presence of God. He is God's greatest Word and he spoke God's word to us. He surpasses Moses, the Law and Wisdom. He is the way and the truth for fullness of human living. He is God's faithful reliable messenger who has come to us and continues to come to us so that we 'may have life and have it abundantly'. His presence, his actions, his words, his suffering and at times his silence give us the privilege of hearing God speak to us.

Now prayerfully hear the assurance that God has spoken and continues to speak to you in Jesus.

God's Messenger

As you meet me in my words, hear my Father say, 'This is my Son the beloved, listen to him.'   *ref: Mk 9:7*

Whoever has seen me has seen the Father. Believe me that I am in the Father and the Father is in me.   *ref: Jn 14:9, 11*

The works that the Father has given me to complete, testify on my behalf that the Father has sent me.   *ref: Jn 5:36*

You have my Father's word abiding in you when you believe in me whom he has sent.   *ref: Jn 5:38*

I do not speak on my own. It is the Father living in me who is doing his work.   *ref: Jn 14:10*

I speak the words of my Father and I give the Spirit without measure. Whoever believes in me has eternal life.   *ref: Jn 3:34-36*

Because you believe in me you hear my Father's voice when you hear my word.   *ref: Jn 5:37, 38*

Now that I have been raised from the dead, believe the scripture and the word I have spoken.   *ref: Jn 2:22*

Blessed are your ears because they hear what the prophets and many good people did not hear.   *ref: Mt 13:16, 17*

In the Old Testament, the king was the one who shepherded his people rather than one who ruled autocratically. In fulfilment of Zechariah's prophecy, Jesus entered Jerusalem seated on a donkey, thus claiming to be a king. Earlier the people had wanted him to be a political king but he refused. On Calvary the priests and Scribes mocked, 'Let the Messiah, the King of Israel come down from the cross now'. One thief, crucified alongside Jesus said, 'Remember me when you come into your kingdom.' Yet Jesus had told Pilate, 'My kingdom is not of this world.'

Jesus assured us that at the end of the world he will be seen coming as a king who will conduct the Last Judgement. Yet the kingdom is already here. Jesus said, 'The kingdom of God is among you', and his miracles demonstrated this. By baptism and faith we are all members of that kingdom. It is described by Paul when he told the Romans that it was a kingdom of 'righteousness, peace and joy in the Holy Spirit'. In so far as we live, work towards, and pray for its coming in its fullness, we are already members of the kingdom.

The church is not identified with the kingdom. The church is called to model it and to build it. The church longs, prays and works for the complete reign of God and it hopes one day to be united in glory with its king. Our first prayer must always be 'Thy Kingdom come.'

More deeply still, Pope John Paul II said, 'The Kingdom of God is not a concept, a doctrine or a programme. Before all else it is a person with the name of Jesus of Nazareth'

Now receive prayerfully the privilege of belonging to and the privilege of building God's Kingdom.

The Kingdom of God

I have rescued you from the power of darkness and transferred you into the kingdom of my beloved Son, in whom you have redemption, the forgiveness of sins.   *ref: Col 1:13*

The coming of my kingdom brings righteousness, peace and joy by the power of my Holy Spirit.   *ref: Rom 14:17*

I have chosen the poor of the world to be rich in faith and to be heirs of the kingdom that I have promised to those who love me.   *ref: Jas 2:5*

Do not be afraid little flock. It was my pleasure to give you my kingdom. Sell your possessions and give alms, for where your treasure is there your heart will also be.   *ref: Lk 12:32-34*

It is when you change and become humble like a child that you enter my kingdom.   *ref: Mt 18:4*

Confirm your call to the kingdom by your goodness, your self-control and affection for all.   *ref: 2 Pet 1:10*

My kingdom is like yeast which gradually leavens the whole world. ref: *Mt 13:33*

In the end, my Son will hand over the kingdom to me after he has destroyed every ruler, every authority, every power, even death itself.   *ref: 1 Cor 15:24-26*

The word missionary often described a person going to a non-Christian country hoping to bring others into the church. This is a seriously limited concept of mission because the entire Church is missionary no matter where it exists. Until a Christian would like to introduce others to Christ, he or she is not yet fully Christian.

To be mission-minded it is of course necessary to have a deep experience of Jesus Christ, which then brings an equally deep urge to tell others about him. It is more an irrepressible desire than a command, just as the experience of any good news urges us to tell others about it.

Mission began when God the Father sent his Son to tell all people about the good news of his love for them. This mission continues by the power of the Holy Spirit in the church through its members. Each of us has a unique mission, many special things to do in order to bring others closer to goodness and to God. And if I fail to do my share, it will never be done. No one else can make my unique contribution.

Strictly speaking, we cannot pass on the faith, only the disposition to receive it. This begins with simple friendship and then helping people in any way we can. Only after this can we speak to them about God. 'Holy' words are meaningless unless they are preceded by human words and actions. There is no reason to become discouraged when family or friends fail to attend Sunday Eucharist. This demands a high level of faith, towards which they may be growing.

Now hear deeply God's personal invitation to fulfil your unique mission.

Mission

I loved you so much that I sent my Son on a mission to mediate my love to you in human form.   *ref: 1 Jn 4:10*

I sent John the Baptiser on his mission to bear witness to my Son, the light to come.   *ref: Jn 1:6, 7*

Mary accepted my mission to become mother of my beloved Son. 'Here I am, the servant of the Lord. Let it be done to me according to your word.'   *ref: Lk 1:38*

Despite his doubts, Joseph too accepted my mission to become the spouse of Mary who was already with child.   *ref: Mt 1:18-25*

My Son Jesus proclaimed his mission publicly in the synagogue at Nazareth .   *ref: Lk 4:16-21*

I have called you also, to be a trustworthy steward of my mysteries.   *ref: 1 Cor 4:1, 2*

Continue to proclaim the good news to all whom you meet.   *ref: Mt 16:15*

Do not proclaim yourself but proclaim me your God who came into the world in the face of Jesus as Lord.   *ref: 2 Cor 4:5-6*

May others observe your teaching, your conduct, your goals in life, your faith, your patience, your love and your steadfastness to the end.   *ref: 2 Tim 3:10*

The prophet Jeremiah has God say, 'Woe to those who build their house by unrighteousness and their upper room by injustice, who make their neighbours work for nothing and do not give them their wages.' To be a friend of God means acting justly towards our neighbour and making an effort to ensure that systems reflect God's justice too.

Jesus was a friend to the rich and to the poor, to those with power and those without it. Yet he was clearly biased in favour of those living on the margin – the poor, the women, the tax collectors, the lepers and the foreigners. If we care to look we can see some individuals or groups marginalised in our local society today. And because of travel and television we have a greater opportunity to see injustice and inequalities in and between countries. Similarly we can observe individual greed enshrined in systems and in laws. The gap between the rich and the poor continues to increase.

The fundamental principle of social justice is that every individual as a child of God has personal and social rights which must be secured so that they can live according to the standards appropriate to human dignity.

In recent years the church leaders and other groups have spoken out strongly in favour of social justice. More Christians have died in pursuit of justice in the past thirty years than in the previous three hundred years. Pope John Paul II said that we have just come through 'a century of martyrs'.

Now, prayerfully accept God's invitation to do what you can to further this integral part of evangelisation.

Social Justice

Even on earth I desire to set up a kingdom of righteousness, peace and joy for all.   *ref: Rom 14:17*

Blessed are you when you hunger and thirst for this rightousness in yourself and in society.   *ref: Mt 5:6*

You are blessed when you create situations in which you are a peacemaker among people.   *ref: Mt 5:9*

To show favouritism to the rich over the poor is a failure to believe in your glorious Lord Jesus Christ. Never dishonour or oppress the poor.   *ref: Jas 2:1-6*

Express your faith in good work for others, for faith alone is dead if not accompanied by good works.   *ref: Jas 2:14-17*

In my name challenge those who impose heavy burdens on people and then fail to lift a finger to move them.   *ref: Mt 23:4*

Seek my wisdom which is pure, peaceable, gentle, willing to yield, full of mercy and good fruits without a trace of partiality or hypocrisy.   *ref: Jas 3:17*

Join me as I scatter the proud, bring down the powerful from their thrones and lift up the lowly.   *ref: Lk 1:52*

Asking for God's help is a common form of prayer. In Gethesmene, Jesus asked for relief from his suffering. He told us to ask in his name so that his Father will be glorified and that when our hearts are united to his, we will get what we ask for. Of course he told us to set our hearts first on his kingdom and then all we need will be given to us. Prayer is more about trust in God and about hope for the coming of his kingdom than about re-arranging the world to suit ourselves.

The prayer of a selfish person makes no sense. An Irish proverb says that when the hand ceases to scatter the heart ceases to pray. Paul told the Corinthians that he asked God for encouragement but only in order to pass it on to them.

Nor is prayer like magic. There is no 'never known to fail' formula. Unless we work as much as we can for something, praying for it is pointless. Prayer can give us more energy to work harder for what we need, rather than deliver a sudden solution. Authentic prayer is harder on the soles of our feet than on our knees. It is the people who work hardest for others who pray best for their welfare.

Writing to the Philippians, Paul offers us wisdom: 'Do not worry about anything, but in everything by prayer and supplication with thanksgiving let your requests be made known to God. And the peace of God which surpasses all understanding will guard your hearts and your minds in Christ Jesus.'

Now, let God's word speak to you deeply about praying for your requests.

Prayer of Petition

Pray in my Spirit at all times. In every prayer and supplication keep alert and pray often in supplication for all believers. *ref: Eph 6:18*

I urge you to make supplication, prayers, intercessions and thanksgiving for everyone. Pray especially for political leaders so that all may live quiet and peaceable lives in godliness and dignity. *ref: 1 Tim 1:1, 2*

When you are suffering you should pray. When you are joyful sing songs of praise. *ref: Jas 5:13*

Pray for all who suffer. The prayer of a good person is very powerful. *ref: Jas 5:13*

Rejoice in hope, be patient in suffering. Persevere in prayer. *ref: Rom 12:13*

Pray that my word will spread rapidly and be glorified everywhere just as it is in you. *ref: 2 Thess 3:1*

Pray every day that my kingdom will come and that my name will be hallowed. *ref: Lk 11:2*

While you pray for blessings give thanks too for blessings received. *ref: 2 Cor 1:11*

Prayer is always time spent on our relationship with God, and so it is possible to pray alone anywhere and in any circumstance. But all Christian prayer involves conscious or subconscious connectedness with the community of the church. Prayer together is a central tradition for God's people.

After returning from the Mount of the Ascension, the disciples 'were constantly devoting themselves to prayer'. In the Acts we read that the community, having prayed together after Peter and John's release were filled with the Holy Spirit.

Praise is central to Christian prayer. The pagans imagined that their gods, like all humans, needed praise or demanded it. They thought that their gods might be more generous or less punitive if they were praised. For the pagans, praise was a bribe or an obligation. Christian praise is entirely different. We sing 'Holy, holy, holy', or 'Alleluia', not because God needs it but because we spontaneously want to do it. For us. praise of God is as spontaneous as when we sincerely say to someone 'You are great!'.

Sometimes our feelings do not support us in prayer; we feel dried up. At these times the use of a favourite formula is very real prayer. Karl Rahner encouragingly reminds us, 'We must quite simply be praying persons who have the courage all our lives, to penetrate, without being clear, into that silent mystery which we call God from whom no response seems to come other than the strength to go on believing, hoping and praying again.'

Now, reflect meditatively on these words of God about prayer of praise together.

Praising God Together

In union with the first Christians, centre your life around the apostles' teaching, fellowship, the breaking of bread and prayer.   *ref: Acts 2:42*

Join the crowd on the path from the Mount of Olives praising my Son with a loud voice.   *ref: Lk 18:37*

Because my good pleasure made you my daughter or my son, you can sing the praise of my glorious grace bestowed on you in my Beloved.   *ref: Eph 1:5-6*

Through Christ, continually offer a sacrifice of praise. Such sacrifices are pleasing to me.   *ref: Heb 13:15-16*

Praise me like the first Christians as they broke bread and ate their food with glad and generous hearts.   *ref: Acts 2:46-47*

Marked with the seal of the promised Holy Spirit as a pledge of your inheritance, you can always sing to the praise of my glory.   *ref: Eph 1:13-14*

One day in heaven, you will join the great multitude singing 'Alleluia! For the Lord our God the Almighty reigns. Let us rejoice and exult and give him the glory'.
ref: Acts 19:6-7

It would be impossible to have our hearts and minds consciously on God at all times. But when we live in faith and act lovingly, our lives are subconsciously lives of prayer. Besides, like all our friendships, our friendship with God needs special times and places set aside for closeness. There is a need to move away from work, to leave the crowd, to go away from noise, just as Jesus did, in order to pray in a more active, conscious, focused and deeper way.

This does not happen automatically; it calls for a decision. It involves the choice of a certain time and of a certain place. This place can be a church, a park, a lakeside, a room or any 'sacred space' you have chosen. Mark tells us that 'in the morning while it was still very dark, Jesus got up and went to a deserted place to pray'. Matthew tells us that during the day, 'after he had dismissed the crowds he went up the mountain by himself to pray'. Matthew also tells us that Jesus prayed in the evening too, and he prayed in preparation for big decisions like choosing his apostles. During his last meal with his friends he prayed for them and for us as future believers. He prayed when he was struggling with faith and doubt and disappointment on the cross.

Although it is increasingly difficult when our lives seem to be getting busier, it is important that we set aside definite times and places for intimate communion with God.

Now ponder over how Jesus managed to do this, as he invites you to do the same.

Times for Prayer

Because the Father and I are one I often stopped my work to pray.   *ref: Jn 10:30*

My ministry began when the Holy Spirit led me into the desert to pray.   *ref: Mt 4:1*

Despite the need of people to hear me and be cured, I would often go apart to pray.   *ref: Lk 5:15-16*

I began and I ended each day alone in conscious prayer to the Father.   *ref: Mk 1:35 and Mt 14:24*

Beginning my public ministry at my baptism, I was praying.   *ref: Lk 3:21*

Before making a serious choice I spent the whole night in prayer.   *ref: Lk 6:12-13*

Under stress to abandon my vocation I sought help in prayer.   *ref: Lk 22:42 and Mt 26:36-39, 27:47*

In agony, fear and doubt I prayed the prayer of surrender.   *ref: Mt 27:47*

Often go into your room and shut the door and pray to your Father in secret.   *ref: Mt 6:6*

The priest philosopher Teilhard de Chardin wrote, 'Some day after mastering the winds, the waves, the tides and gravity, we shall harness for God the energies of love, and then, for the second time in the history of the world, man will discover fire.' However, the word love has had, and continues to have, many meanings in human usage.

The most common Hebrew word for love in the Old Testament is *aheb*. It meant to love a friend or to like food. It was also used to describe God's love for us but the text adds 'with an everlasting love' to show that God's love is different because of its fidelity.

When another Hebrew word *hesed* was used for love, it always implied a relationship of loving kindness with emphasis on mercy. Moses hears that God abounds in *hesed*. God's love in the Old Testament is portrayed as a love which selects Israel in a special way to be a witness, and to mediate his love to other nations. God often laments Israel's failure to return love, 'I remember the devotion of your youth, your love as a bride, how you followed me in the wilderness.'

God's love is infinite and unconditional. God not only loves, but as St John tells us, God *is* love. The model of mutual love in the Old Testament was 'Love your neighbour as yourself', but Jesus calls us to another level of loving: 'Love one another as I have loved you'. The standard for loving has changed.

Now ponder prayerfully on the words of Jesus giving you the model, the source and offering you the privilege of loving others.

Loving Others

I love you as the Father loves me. Abide in my love. I have told you this so that my own joy may be in you and your be joy complete.'   *ref: Jn 15:9, 11*

Have genuine mutual love. Love one another deeply from the heart.   *ref: 1 Pet 1:22*

Like good stewards of my grace, serve one another with whatever gift you have received.   *ref: 1 Pet 4:10*

Have unity of spirit, sympathy and love for one another, and always endeavour to repay abuse with a blessing.
ref: 1 Pet 3:8

Never seek only your own interests but rather show genuine concern for all.   *ref: Phil 2:19-24*

Bless those who persecute you. Live in harmony and associate with the lowly.   *ref: Rom 12:16*

Never command favours from friends. Rather appeal to their love for you.   *ref: Philem 8-10*

One day I will reassure you that what you did for every one of my least, you did for me.   *ref: Mt 25:40*

The deepest experience of our lives is to know that we are loved and the fundamental experience of the Christian life is to know that one is loved by God. In his first letter to the church, Pope Benedict XVI reminds us that when we say that we are loved by God and really believe it, we are expressing the fundamental decision of our Christian lives. It is the beginning of everything else. He says that it is only after this experience that we can love God and love one another.

The Greeks used the word *eros* to express genuine love as between spouses, but it is a love that has a degree of self-interest; it is not totally selfless loving. It is love that depends to some degree on the reward of enjoying the other person.

The New Testament speaks of *agape* which means totally selfless love. *Eros*-love can be the beginning of this completely self-giving *agape*-love, and it becomes identified with it when it is purified. *Eros*-love is selective while *agape*-love is unconditional and universal.

We all need to experience *eros*-love from those close to us. This is because it would be impossible to live the high demands of totally selfless *agape*-love without some experience of already being loved however imperfectly. We need to feel loved, if we in turn are to give it.

Authentic Christian love begins in the experience and acceptance of the fact that we are loved unconditionally by God. It then flows through us when we decide to act lovingly towards others.

Now, meditatively listen to Jesus tell you how love of God and of others are one.

Loving Others

My final prayer to my Father was my desire that my love
for him and his love for me may be in all my disciples.
ref: Jn 17:26

No one has ever seen my Father, but if you love others he
will live in you and his love be perfected in you.   *ref: 1 Jn 4:12*

Whoever fails to love does not know the Father, because
my Father is love.   *ref: 1 Jn 7:8*

I give you a new commandment. Just as I have loved you,
you also should love one another. Then everyone will
know that you are my disciple.   *ref: Jn 13:34-35*

Washing my apostles' feet is a model for your service for
others.   *ref: Jn 13:15*

Love one another since love comes from me and everyone
who loves is a child of God and knows God.   *ref: 1 Jn 4:7*

If you fail to love your brother or sister whom you can see
how can you love my Father and I whom you cannot see?
ref: 1 Jn 4:20

The sign that you have passed from death to life is that you
love one another as God loves you.   *ref: 1 Jn 3:14*

To the Galatian community Paul wrote, 'The only thing that matters is faith working through love.' To the Roman community he said that 'God's love has been poured into our hearts.' Paul is telling us that this gift of loving comes to us as power, as energy from the Holy Spirit. God's love is not something static; it is dynamic.

Nor is love just an experience to be relished; it is an experience to be passed on. God's love is not just to us; not just within us; it is through us or it is not present at all. Love then is not merely a matter of morality, not just a command but a gift flowing through us. Our love for God and our love for others can never be separated.

Love is not a matter of feeling, of enjoying another person. Feelings come and go; they cannot be commanded; they react instinctively and cannot be directly controlled. Love is different. Whether we are aware of it or not, love is a decision to use the power of God within us to enhance another person. If I enjoy you it is because *you* are an enjoyable person, but if I love you it is because *I* am a loving person.

A Christian community or parish or the world church is a group of people who have received and who pour out God's love on one another. For Paul it is joining the flow of love within the Trinity and it is God's future breaking into the present. Love never ends.

Now, be aware that praying on God's words about love can yield a rich harvest in you.

Loving Others

Pour out my love which has been poured into your heart by the Holy Spirit whom you have received. *ref: Rom 5:5.*

I continue to dwell in your heart through faith as you are being rooted and grounded in love. *ref: Eph 3:17*

I have placed a variety of gifts in my church because there is a variety of services to be done. *ref: 1 Cor 12:4*

Love is patient, kind, not arrogant or rude nor does it insist on its own way. *ref: 1 Cor 13:4-5*

Love is not irritable or resentful. It does not rejoice in wrongdoing but rejoices only in the truth. *ref: 1 Cor 13:5-6*

Welcome one another as Christ has welcomed you.   *ref: Rom 15:7*

Rejoice with those who rejoice and weep with those in sorrow. *ref: Rom 12:15*

If you have faith to move mountains but lack love, you are a noisy gong or a clanging cymbal. *ref: 1 Cor 13:1-3*

Faith, hope and love abide, and the greatest of these is love. *ref: 1 Cor 13:13*

The Hebrew word for sin means missing the mark. This reminded God's people that their lives must be accurately centred, unerringly directed towards union with God. It was possible to go off this target.

In the Old Testament, believers saw sin as disobedience to God's Law, a law which expressed God's loving guidance. Sin disrupted God's gracious purpose for their growth towards wholeness and goodness.

In his final discourse, Jesus said that only the Holy Spirit can enlighten us to the true nature of sin, 'When he comes he will prove the world wrong about sin ... because they do not believe in me.' Sin is a failure in faith; it is a full or partial refusal to accept Jesus as the complete revelation of God. In his first letter John writes, 'No one who remains in him (Christ) sins and whoever sins has neither seen him or recognised him.' The more we experience God's love in Christ the less we sin.

In John's gospel Jesus also tells us that sin is loss of freedom: 'Very truly I tell you, everyone who commits sin is a slave to sin.' When we sin we are refusing the salvation or freedom offered by God and so inflicting self-harm. St. Thomas Aquinas confirms this when he writes, 'We do not offend God unless we harm ourselves.' Rather than seeing sin as offending God we could perhaps understand it as making God sad because his child is becoming less free, less loving, less God-like.

Now, pray slowly over God's word to you on the tragedy of sin in our lives.

Sin

My Spirit has revealed sin's origin. It is failure to believe deeply in me and that I have come from God.   *ref: Jn 16:8-9*

The law of the Spirit of life in my Son sets you free from the law of sin and death.   *ref: Rom 8:2*

Everyone who commits sin is a slave to sin. But if my Sonmakes you free you will be free indeed.   *ref: Jn 8:34-36*

The wages of sin is death but my free gift is eternal life in my Son.   *ref: Rom 6:23*

I know that often you cannot understand your own actions. You know what is right but cannot do it. You fail to do the good you want to do but the evil you do not want, you do.   *ref: Rom 7:15-20*

Wretched as you might feel, I can rescue you from this body of death through my Son Jesus Christ.   *ref: Rom 7:24, 25*

When you confess your sins, I who am faithful and just will forgive you and cleanse you from all evil.   *ref: 1 Jn 1:9*

Your old self has been crucified with my Son. You no longer need to be enslaved to sin. Having died to sin how could you go on living in it?   *ref: Rom 6:2-6*

In their experience of God throughout the Old Testament, the chosen people continually described God with the word *hesed*, meaning faithful forgiving love despite their failures.

In Luke's gospel Jesus describes God as a loving father whose younger son demands half of his inheritance while his father is still alive. The loving father respects his son's foolish choice and allows him to leave home to live a dissolute life. Later, because the boy found himself penniless and starving he decided to return home. While still a long way off the merciful father saw his emaciated son and ran to meet him. He embraced him lovingly and kissed him. He did not reprimand him or ask any questions.

The father's forgiveness was always present because he had never condemned his son. The wayward boy had only to return and accept his father's forgiveness. No punishment was given. The father was so happy to receive him home that he invited him to join with his family and friends in a welcoming party with choice meat, music and dancing.

The boy's elder brother who had never left home, apparently made a bigger mistake; he complained that he had 'slaved' for his father over many years, believing that he had to earn his father's love. For this reason he was angry towards his father and resented his brother being welcomed home. Unlike him, let us remind ourselves that God's forgiveness is always there even before we ask it. We have only to accept it by acknowledging our sins and then to celebrate when we receive it.

Now, listen prayerfully to the gift of mercy offered to you always, and rejoice in God your Saviour.

Forgiven

I am the Father of mercies and the God of all consolation.
ref: 2 Cor 1:3

My mercy is from generation to generation for those who revere me. *ref: Lk 1:50*

I am the Father who never condemns and who always welcomes you home. *ref: Rom 8:1 and Lk 15:11-24*

In my Son you have forgiveness for your sins. He has lavished the riches of his grace upon you. *ref: Eph 1:7*

When you confess your sins and accept my mercy you are forgiven and cleansed from all unrighteousness. *ref: 1 Jn 1:9*

My invitation to you is not to sin, but if you do, my Son is your advocate with me. *ref: 1 Jn 2:1-2*

I ask you to live in gratitude because I rescued you from the power of darkness and into the kingdom of my Son.In him you have redemption – your sins forgiven. *ref: Col 1:13-14*

By my tender mercy the dawn from on high has broken upon you, giving you light in darkness and in the shadow of death, guiding your feet into the way of peace. *ref: Lk 1:77-79*

Rejoice in me, God your Saviour. *ref: Lk 1:47*

It is not our minds which first react when we are offended. It is not even our desire to defend ourselves or to strike back. It is our feelings which respond first as they react instantly to hurtful words or actions. We immediately feel pain, sadness, anger or disappointment, and these negative feelings can remain a long time whether we wish them to or not. Feelings do not forgive easily, no matter how much we desire them to. For this reason, real forgiveness has little to do with feelings over which we have little direct control.

Yet Jesus asks that we continually forgive one another just as God endlessly forgives us. Forgiveness is therefore not a feeling; it a choice, a decision. Your answers to the following questions will tell how deep your forgiveness is. Do you refrain from wishing evil on the other person? If you do, this is a deep beginning of forgiveness. Would you refrain from hurting the other person? This is another important step. If the other person were in dire need, would you help? When you are ready to do this it is yet more evidence that you have forgiven – in spite of your hurt feelings. If you could spontaneously offer help to or ask for help from the person who hurt you, you have reached a high level of forgiveness. Whichever of these levels you can manage for the moment is the forgiveness God asks of you when you are offended. Refusing to offer forgiveness could make one unworthy to approach the Eucharist.

Listen deeply now and hear all this in God's own words.

Forgiving

In imitation of my unconditional love, I invite you to be like me your heavenly Father, perfect in merciful loving. *ref: Mt 5:38-48*

Your forgiveness must imitate mine, forgiving seventy seven times – endlessly. *ref: Mt 18:21-22*

Imitate me, bear with others' weaknesses and forgive them as I forgive you. Be clothed in my peace and in my love. *ref: Col 3:12-15*

Put away all bitterness and wrath, all anger, wrangling, slander and malice, forgiving others as my Son forgave you. *ref: Eph 4:31-32*

When offended unite yourself with my Son and say 'Father forgive them, they do not know what they are doing.' *ref: Lk 23:34*

When you stand in prayer forgive those you have anything against. *ref: Mk 11:25*

Before you offer gifts at my altar, offer reconciliation to those who have something against you. *ref: Mt 5:23-24*

Mercy given assures mercy received. *ref: Mt 5:7*

The Old Testament uses the Hebrew word *basar* for flesh or for the body, and it is often used synonymously with weakness. This weakness and our mortality give us one perspective on humanity. Because we are flesh we are weak, frail and mortal. The history of God's chosen people is one of strength and weakness, of success and failure in keeping the covenant.

In both Testaments it is recognised that without the power and energy which comes from God, we will behave less than ideally. Even a deep desire for goodness cannot always result in good behaviour. We depend on God and God asks us to live with an awareness of this dependence. God does not remove our humanity or our weakness. We are not God. Even with God's help we still remain weak but he always offers us the power to overcome evil.

When Paul complained about his weakness, God told him, 'My grace is sufficient for you, for power is made perfect in weakness.' Finally, to the Corinthians he was able to say that he could boast of his weaknesses so that the power of Christ might dwell in him.

God also asks us to understand the weakness of others and to encourage one another on our journey. Compassion for one's own weakness and for that of others is central to the Christian life. A believer is always willing to suffer with and to support the weakness of the other. To be Christian is to *be-long* to others in this way.

Now prayerfully ponder on these encouraging words of God to you in your weakness.

Human Weakness

Always try to stay awake and to pray in time of trial. Your spirit is strong but your flesh is weak.   *ref: Mt 26:41*

I chose what is weak in the world to shame the strong, so that no one can boast in my presence.   *ref: 1 Cor 1:27-29*

When you are tempted my grace is sufficient, for power is made perfect in weakness. Be content with your weakness for when you are weak you are strong.   *ref: 2 Cor 12:7-10*

When you are strong be patient with the failings of the weak.   *ref: Rom 15:1*

Welcome those who are weak in faith because I welcome them, and I can make them stand.   *ref: Rom 14:1-4*

Admonish idlers, encourage the faint-hearted, help the weak and have patience with all.   *ref: 1 Thess 5:14*

My glory which shone in the face of Christ shines in your heart. But you have this treasure in a fragile clay jar. This extraordinary power belongs to me.   *ref: 2 Cor 4:6-7*

What is sown is perishable, what is raised is imperishable. Your body was sown in weakness. I will raise it in power one day.   *ref: 1 Cor 15:42-44*

Encouragement is one of the most noble and effective ways to help another person to grow and to appreciate themselves. When we are encouraged, we are motivated and moved to do our best, especially in demanding situations. The Hebrew word translated as encouragement also means to strengthen.

In the New Testament the word-group *paraklesis,* which is translated as encouragement, occurs over one hundred times. Because the Holy Spirit is called the Paraclete, we are reminded that encouragement is the work of the Holy Spirit. The word can also mean to invite, to ask, to exhort or to comfort. In the New Testament the main purpose of encouragement is that we may be strengthened in our faith-struggle, in fidelity to God's call.

In the Acts of the Apostles, 1st Thessalonians and 2nd Corinthians, the Good News itself is regarded as the main source of encouragement. In his second letter to believers in Thessalonica, Paul reminds them that God's grace and love encourage our hearts and strengthen us in every good deed and word.

In Acts and in Paul's writings, to encourage another implies speaking in God's name with the power of the Holy Spirit. To give encouragement is one of the functions of preaching. Paul said that he received encouragement from Lydia's family and from Philemon's love. The church exists in miniature and in its essence where two or three believers encourage each other in faith.

Now, prayerfully enjoy God's constant offer of, and his call to practise, encouragement of others in your life.

Encouragement

I am the God of steadfastness and encouragement who through the scriptures gives you hope. *ref: Rom 15:4-5*

Through others, I speak to you for your upbuilding, encouragement and consolation. *ref: 1 Cor 14:3; Acts 15:32*

Those who proclaim my gospel can strengthen and encourage one another in faith. *ref: 1 Thess 3:2*

As you communicate lovingly with others, you offer them refreshing joy and encouragement. *ref: Philem 7*

I ask you to encourage especially the fainthearted and to build one another up. *ref: 1 Thess 4:18; 5:11*

In times of trial, you have my power to encourage. *ref: Acts 16:40*

I urge you to proclaim my message with persistence. Convince, rebuke and encourage, but do it with patience. *ref: 2 Tim 4:1-2*

Encourage others to lead a life worthy of me who calls each one into my kingdom and glory. *ref: 1 Thess 2:11-12*

Encourage friends to meet together for prayer. *ref: Heb 10:24-25*

I, the God of steadfastness and encouragement, will grant you to live in harmony with others, so that together you may glorify me your Father in heaven. *ref: Rom 15:5-6*

Using the Greek word *metanoia*, the Old Testament gives many examples of both God and people having repented about something they did and then changed their minds. In the book of Samuel we read that God repented having made Saul king of Israel. However, the rabbis used the word to express changing one's mind about an evil life. God's people were constantly called on to repent by moving away from sin and towards living the Covenant. The hope is expressed that the Messiah would lead all people to God by conversion.

In the New Testament, repentance – *metanoia* – still means taking a new direction in one's life. John the Baptist, Jesus and Peter began their ministry with a call for a deep conversion, an inner change. This is both a gift from God and a task to undertake. It is a recognition that of myself and by myself I tend to go in the wrong direction. This is followed by my willingness to co-operate with God in changing that direction.

In this sense, although it can involve an initial deep decision, it is also a process constantly undertaken. It is not just a change in my behaviour. It is a constant redirecting of my heart, of my attitude towards God. That includes a decision constantly renewed, to turn away from my own ways to the ways of God, from sin towards holiness. For this reason it is a consequence of faith; it is built into my decision to believe in God's love for me.

Now, prayerfully receive and reflect on God's call to continual repentance in your life.

Repentance

John the Baptist began his ministry in preparation for my coming with the words 'Repent for the kingdom of heaven has come near.'   *ref: Mt 3:1-2*

The first words of my mission were also an invitation to repent, to change, to turn to me and tobelieve the good news.   *ref: Mk 1:15*

Peter's ministry too began with the invitation 'Repent and turn to God so that your sins may be wiped out.'   *ref: Acts 3:19*

I invite you to continually change toward the simplicity, spontaneity and sincerity of a child.   *ref: Mt 18:3*

I invite you to continue turning from darkness to light to receive forgiveness and holiness through faith in me.   *ref: Acts 26:18*

Turn away from evil and do good. Always seek peace and pursue it.   *ref: 1 Pet 3:11*

Repent and turn to me so that my presence will bring you times of refreshment.   *ref: Acts 3:20*

I send you to proclaim the same repentance and forgiveness of sin to all whom you meet.   *ref: Lk 24:47-49*

WEEK TWO

Only by the light of faith and by meditation on the Word of God
- can one always and everywhere recognise God in whom we live, move and exist
- seek his will in every event
- see Christ in all persons, whether they be close to us or strangers, and make correct judgements about the true meaning and value of things, both in themselves and in their relations to our final goal.

Vatican Council II, *Decree on the Laity*, 11

The Hebrew word for holiness, *qadas,* means something apart, separated from what might be imperfect or impure. It is used to describe the goodness, the greatness and the majesty of God. It also describes the person who is morally good. The verb – to become holy – means to become consecrated, to be dedicated, to be set apart. It describes persons, places, times and things set apart for God. For instance, the nation of Israel was holy; the seventh day was holy; Mount Sinai was holy and the priests were expected to be holy in order to carry out holy rituals.

During his Last Supper prayer, Jesus addresses his Father as holy and asks him to make his apostles holy in the truth. The church is the new Israel and it is holy in the sense of being chosen by God and set apart for him. Christians are expected to live holy lives, to act lovingly towards others by the power of the Holy Spirit and to use holy rites in their worship. In his first letter Peter says, 'As he who called you is holy, be holy yourselves in all your conduct.'

We have all met saintly people who stand out as better than most of us, and we have the inspiration of the recognised saints who have exemplified holiness in an extraordinary way. Luke tells us that Jesus 'increased in wisdom and in years, and in human and divine favour'. Human holiness reached its perfection in him.

Only in prayer will you hear God describe divine holiness which is reflected in the holiness of Jesus and again in your own call to holiness.

The Holiness of God

I am the almighty one and holy is my name.   *ref: Lk 1:49*

Join the angels singing 'holy, holy, holy, the Lord God the Almighty, who was, and is and is to come'.   *ref: Rev 4:4, 8*

Jesus my Son is my holy one.   *ref: Jn 6:69*

He is the high priest, holy, blameless, undefiled, separated from sinners and exalted above the heavens.   *ref: Heb 7:26*

In him I chose you to be holy and blameless before me in love.   *ref: Eph 1:4*

In his body he has reconciled you to me so that he could present you holy and blameless and irreproachable before him.   *ref: Col 1:21-22*

In him you are called into my household, growing into my holy temple, a dwelling place for me.   *ref: Eph 2:19-22*

As my chosen one, holy and beloved, clothe yourself with compassion, kindness, humility, meekness and patience. *ref: Col 3:12*

I appeal to you by my mercy to present your body as a living sacrifice in spiritual worship, holy and acceptable to me.   *ref: Rom 12:1*

The words light and darkness pervade most religions, where they are often metaphors for good and for evil. In some Greek cults, light was thought to drive out demons. In the Old Testament, light and darkness were mostly described as places. Light was connected to God or salvation, and darkness to the absence of God or perdition. In the first book of Genesis God is portrayed as a person who brings light out of darkness, creation out of chaos. God said, 'Let there be light and there was light, and God saw that light was good and God separated the light from the darkness'.

God helped Moses to meet him in the light of the burning bush, and God led his people Israel, with a pillar of fire on their journey. Light is a manifestation of God in action, and God's light makes what is hidden visible. The Psalmist said to God, 'With you is the fountain of light, and in your light we see light.' The prophet Isaiah foretold that in the end God will be Israel's eternal light, and that nations will come to that light.

In the Book of Revelation heaven is described as a place where there will be no more night and no more need for sunlight or lamps, because God will be our light forever. Luke, Paul and Peter all speak of two empires, one of Christ and one of Satan. People choose to be either 'children of light' or 'children of darkness'.

Now in your prayer, let the light of God come more deeply into your soul.

God is Light

I, your God have immortality and I dwell in unapproachable light.   *ref: 1 Tim 6:16*

Once you were in darkness but now in me you are light. Let no one deceive you with empty words. Live as a child of the light.   *ref: Eph 5:8*

I said 'Let light shine out of darkness' and now I shine in your heart to give you the light of the knowledge of my glory, in the face of my Son.   *ref: 2 Cor 4:6*

In me you have been rescued from the power of darkness and transferred into the kingdom of my beloved Son in whom you have forgiveness of sins.'   *ref: Col 1:13-14*

The fruit of this light is found in all that is good and right and true. Take no part in the unfruitful works of darkness. *ref: Eph 5:9-11*

Let your light shine before others so that they may see your good works and give glory to me your Father in heaven. *ref: Mt 5:16*

Give thanks to me who has enabled you to share in the inheritance of the saints in light.'   *ref: Col 1:12*

In the Old Testament the Hebrew word *raham* means to love deeply, and thus to be compassionate. It was used to describe the depth of God's love for his people. The English word compassion comes from two Latin words – *cum* and *patiar* – together meaning to share another's suffering.

In the New Testament, the Greek word *splanchnon* – translated compassion – describes a human emotion, a deep-felt physical pain at the discomfort of the other. This is the word used to describe God's compassion for us. It is the central message of the New Testament as Jesus tells us, 'be compassionate as your heavenly Father is compassionate.'

Jesus feels and shows compassion for the confused crowds, for lepers and for a widow. And to describe God's compassion for us he tells us about a father's deep joy when he saw his starving son coming home emaciated and in rags. An example of the call to have compassion is given by Jesus when he spoke about the Samaritan who showed compassion to the injured man by the wayside. The Samaritan had three reasons for passing by – the injured man may have been a Jew, touching blood would lead to impurity and because he himself was travelling to a destination. He is the model for loving beyond the borders of personal feelings, culture, race and time.

Paul uses the word compassion in very personal passages showing his affection for others. In one reference he tells his Philippian friends, 'I long for all of you with the compassion of Jesus Christ.'

Now let your heart burn within you like the apostles listening to Jesus on their way to Emmaus, as you accept God's compassionate love for you.

God is Compassion

I your God, am a compassionate Father, compassionate and merciful.   *ref: Lk 6:36 and Jas 5:11*

In my Son who is my compassion, the dawn from on high has broken upon you.   *ref: Lk 1:78*

Through my Son I have compassion on you when your eyes need to be opened.   *ref: Mt 20:32-33*

I have compassion on you when you are blind, sad or sinful.   *ref: Mt 20:34; Lk 7:13; 15:20*

I am moved with compassion when you are harassed, helpless and leaderless.   *ref: Mt 9:36*

I feel compassion for the hungry of today's world and I ask you to help them.   *ref: Mk 8:2-8*

Love others with the compassion of my Son, so that their love too may overflow.   *ref: Phil 1:8-9*

As one of my chosen, holy and beloved, clothe yourself with compassion and kindness, with humility, meekness and patience.   *ref: Col 3:12*

I ask you to long and care for one another with the compassion and sympathy of my Son.   *ref: Phil 1:8; 2:1*

Be compassionate as I your Father am compassionate. Give good measure and it will be given to you. The measure you give is the measure you will receive.   *ref: Lk 6:36-38*

In the Old Testament, through his gifts of Wisdom and the Law, God lighted the way for his people. Each year they acted out this truth at the Feast of Tabernacles, when four seven-branched lampstands lit up part of the temple. As a faithful Jew, Jesus had often taken part in this ceremony.

On his last visit to the temple, Jesus claimed to be replacing these ceremonies of light. He declared that he was the true light of the world, and he asked his followers to radiate this light in the world. John records Jesus saying directly, 'I am the light of the world. Whoever follows me will never walk in darkness but will have the light of life.'

In the beginning of his gospel, John speaks of the Word and states, 'What has come into being in him was life, and that life was the light of all people. The light shines in the darkness, and the darkness did not overcome it … The true light, which enlightens everyone, was coming into the world.'

In his first letter, John warns us, 'Whoever says, I am in the light while hating a brother or sister is still in the darkness. Whoever loves a brother or sister lives in the light.'

The light of Christ is not something that lights up the way around or ahead of us. It is the person in whom we live. The more we walk in the light by Christ-like living, the more light we receive.

Now, slowly and prayerfully walk in the words of God which will always give you light.

Christ our Light

I, Jesus, came into the world so that when you believe in me you will not remain in darkness.   *ref: Jn 12:46*

I am the light of the world. When you follow me you will never walk in darkness. You will have the light of life.
ref: Jn 8:12

My Father sent me as a light into the world, so that everyone who believes in me should not remain in darkness.
ref: Jn 12:46

Those who do what it true come into the light. It is clearly seen that their deeds have been done in God.   *ref: Jn 3:21*

Only those whose deeds are evil love the darkness. They do not come into the light lest their deeds may be exposed.
ref: Jn 3:20-21

I am the true light which enlightens everyone.   *ref: Jn 1:9*

The life I offer is the light of all people, a light that darkness did not overcome.   *ref: Jn 1:4-5*

If you walk in darkness, you do not know where you are going.   *ref: Jn 12:35*

While you have the light, believe in the light, so that you may remain a child of the light.   *ref: Jn 12:36*

For the ancient Greeks as for most of us, hope gave comfort in time of sorrow or distress. Yet they considered it rather risky to hope unless they had consulted a wise person. Plato extended hope rather vaguely to another life where things would be perfect.

In the Old Testament, it was not a neutral hope for a vague future; it was a hope for the triumph of goodness. It was linked to desire and confidence, and was distinct from anxiety and fear. A good life gave grounds for a realistic hope in another life.

In the New Testament faith and hope are closely linked. In Hebrews, we read, 'Faith is the assurance of things hoped for, the conviction of things not seen.' This hope is rooted in Christ's word and is vindicated by his resurrection. It means looking forward with confidence and patient endurance.

The main difference from the hope of the Old Testament is that hope is now founded on faith in Christ. We know that Christ will never desert or disappoint those who have loved, trusted, hoped in and followed him. His kingdom is already within us and among us. In hope we look forward to its final flowering and fulfilment at the end of time.

Our hope rests on the certainty that Christ has risen and has won our salvation. In Colossians, Paul says that our faith is a mystery and that this mystery is 'Christ in us, the hope of glory.' A traditional expression of faith and hope is, 'Christ has died. Christ is risen. Christ will come again.'

Now listen deeply to God offering you the solid ground for your hope.

Christ our Hope

I, your God and Father have given you a new birth into a living hope through the resurrection of my Son from the dead and into an inheritance that is imperishable, undefiled and unfading, kept in heaven for you.   *ref: 1 Pet 3:4*

Through my Son you have come to trust in me who raised him from the dead and gave him glory, so that your faith and hope are set on me.   *ref: 1 Pet 1:21*

My Son will not break the bruised reed or quench a smouldering wick until he brings justice to victory. In his name all people will hope.   *ref: Mt 12:20-21*

He and I your Father who love you, give you eternal comfort and good hope and we strengthen you in every good work and word.   *ref: 2 Thess 2:16-17*

Jesus my Son was faithful over my house. As my child you are part of his house if you hold firm the confidence and the pride that belong to hope.   *ref: Heb 3:6*

The Spirit has been poured out richly on you through my Son, your Saviour. Justified by his grace you have become an heir to the hope of eternal life.   *ref: Ti. 3:6-7*

Having set your hope on my Son, live for the praise of his glory.   *ref: Eph 1:12*

Usually the word truth is connected with telling the truth, but in the Old Testament, truth meant something solid, and when it referred to a person it meant that he or she was a person of integrity.

However, in the New Testament its meaning goes much deeper. John uses the word *aletheia* to mean what is true and authentic, that is what God has revealed and ultimately God's own self.

For John, Jesus speaks the truth, which means that not only what he says is true but that his words reveal God to those receiving them. For John, the words of Jesus open our hearts to the endlessly rich depths of truth in God.

More deeply still Christ is the Truth, and at the Last Supper he prayed for his apostles that God would 'sanctify them in the truth'. The truth which Jesus offers reveals God to believers. The Holy Spirit is 'the spirit of truth' and Jesus tells us to 'worship in spirit and in truth'.

In his first letter John tells us that acceptance of Truth, of Christ, eliminates false doctrine and brings us to a right way of life.

John opens his second letter by saying that he loves his friends in the truth, and that all those who love the truth, naturally love one another. He assures believers that real freedom comes from the truth, that truth abides in us, and that it will be with us forever. In his third letter he calls Christians his 'fellow workers in the truth'.

Now, slowly, allow the depth of the words recorded by John to enter and to permeate your life.

Christ the Truth

In my flesh I am my Father's glory, the glory as of his only Son, I am full of grace and of truth.   *ref: Jn 1:14*

The law was given through Moses, but grace and truth come through me.   *ref: Jn 1:17*

I came into the world to testify to the truth. Everyone who belongs to the truth listens to my voice.   *ref: Jn 18:37*

I am the way, and the truth, and the life. If you know me you know my Father also.   *ref: Jn 14:6-7*

I have sent you another Advocate to be with you forever. He is the Spirit of truth whom the world cannot receive.   *ref: Jn 14:17*

There are many things I did not speak about in my lifetime. Now the Spirit of truth guides you into all truth.   *ref: Jn 16:12-14*

I sanctified myself so that you also may be sanctified in truth.   *ref: Jn 17:17-19*

If you continue in my word, you are truly my disciple, and you will know the truth and the truth will make you free.   *ref: J 8:31-32*

God always desired his people to be a community of faith and love. In the Old Testament this community was a desert people that saw God's wonders and inherited God's promises. The Lord asked them to believe in and to pass on these promises. The Greek word *synagogue* was later used for all God's people, but gradually became centred on the building and its focus was the Law.

The New Testament uses another Greek word *ekklesia* for God's community or the church. Paul wrote about the church and about local churches, the core belief of which was always their recognition of Christ as Lord. This made it distinct from the synagogue especially when the Christians were made unwelcome.

In later letters to the Colossians and Ephesians a more precise doctrine of the church emerges. It is Christ's body with Christ as its head. It is called on to reflect the holiness of Christ who is sanctifying it. In his first letter to Timothy, Paul writes about 'the household of God which is the church of the living God, the pillar and bulwark of the truth'. The New Testament church is the fulfilled Old Testament assembly which is sanctified by Christ. At the end of Galatians, Paul speaks of the Church as 'the Israel of God', and Ephesians speaks of 'the household of God.'

Earliest writings speak of the specific gifts of each member of the church, while at the same time the leadership of bishops, priests and deacons was unfolding. In more recent times these gifts express themselves in roles and responsibilities of every adult in the church.

Now, listen prayerfully to God's ideal for his church and your role in it.

The Church

The Church is my household, the Church of the living God, the pillar and bulwark of the truth.   *ref: 1 Tim 3:15*

Ask the Holy Spirit to guide my church into all truth, so that my Son and I may be glorified today.   *ref: Jn 16:13*

There are a variety of gifts in my church. Each person has a manifestation of the Spirit for the common good.
ref: 1 Cor 12:4-11

Implore the Holy Spirit to set apart apostolic people for the work to which I have called them.   *ref: Acts 13:2*

Work so that the church will build up the reign of God, a reign of righteousness, peace and joy brought by the Holy Spirit.   *ref: Rom 14:17*

Pray that the leaders of my church be filled with my Spirit and with my wisdom.   *ref: Acts 6:3*

Also that they watch over themselves and over the flock of which the Holy Spirit has made them overseers.   *ref: Acts 20:28*

Pray that my church will have peace, be built up and live in the comfort of my Holy Spirit.   *ref: Acts 9:31*

Authority and leadership are often identified with status, power and wealth. Leadership has often been exercised in a way that exploited and dominated people. God's authority is different. In contrast, God emptied himself and became powerless in Jesus.

In the letter to the Philippians we read that the only power God used in Jesus was the power of powerless loving. Jesus used authority as service, not as power. He knew that his authority came from God and made visible God's loving service to his people, guiding them to happiness.

He explained this when he said that he came to serve, not to be served, and that his apostles must never lord it over the people. When his apostles argued about status among themselves, Jesus said that the leader must be like him, one who serves. Finally he gave them a profound visual lesson in Christian leadership when he washed their feet and told them to do the same for others.

When the church became settled and communities could no longer depend on travelling preachers, the local community leader was called *presbyteros* or *episkopos*. The precise meaning of these secular terms is not clear. Their role was to guide, teach, and conduct worship within the Christian community. These community leaders were called by the Holy Spirit in and through the community, and then appointed by the laying on of hands.

God may be offering you a vocation to leadership at some level in the church. Listen deeply as you receive the word and pray often for the leaders of the church.

Christian Leadership

As trustworthy stewards of my mysteries, I have commissioned the leaders of my church to make my word fully known.   *ref: Col 1:25-26 and 1 Cor 4:1, 2*

Pray that they have a firm grasp of my word, able to preach it with sound doctrine and to refute those who contradict it.   *ref: Tit 1:9*

Pray too that they proclaim the message whether the time is favourable or unfavourable – convincing, rebuking and encouraging with utmost patience in teaching.   *ref: 2 Tim 3:2*

Leaders in my church must not choose high places or ask to be served. Pray that they will know they are called to serve.   *ref: Mt 20:24-28 and Jn 13:12-17*

They must be hospitable, lovers of goodness, prudent, upright, devout and self-controlled. I never want them to be arrogant, quick tempered or greedy for gain.   *ref: Tit 1:7-8*

I ask them not to be quarrelsome but kind to everyone, apt teachers, patient and correcting with gentleness.
ref: 2 Tim 2:24

May their greatest joy be to see the faithful walking in my truth.   *ref: 2 Jn 1:4.*

We all like to tell our friends about our pleasant or unpleasant experiences especially if we think the telling will help them.

The Greek Old Testament word for one who recounts an experience, who testifies or who witnesses is *martys*. The *martys* was one who remembered what he or she had experienced and told others about it. They were speaking about something in which they were involved, not just something they had seen. The good person who suffered calumny or even death for courageously speaking the truth was familiar in the history of Israel.

In the New Testament Paul encourages all believers in faithfulness, by pointing to Jesus' witnessing to the truth before Pilate. John speaks mostly of witnessing, not to the facts of Jesus' history, but to the person and significance of Jesus himself in the life of the believer.

In the second century, the *martys* was a person who risked or lost his or her life for witnessing in word or action to their faith.

We cannot give faith to others, but we can help them towards readiness to receive it. This is an important and encouraging thought for parents today. We all have the opportunity to be witnesses as we live out our faith by loving others as Jesus did,. We do this also by carrying out the duties of our way of life, by simply speaking about God to others and by attending the Eucharist. Simple phrases like 'Thank God', 'God willing' or promising to pray for others are small but unmistakable acts of witness.

Listen prayerfully now to Christ speaking to you about witnessing.

Witness

Pour over the scriptures in which you will find eternal life. They witness on my behalf.   *ref: Jn 5:39*

For this I was born; for this I came into the world, to witness to the truth.   *ref: Jn 18:37*

The Baptist came as a witness to me who am the light that enlightens everyone.   *ref: Jn 1:7-9*

The Holy Spirit first descended on my apostles who became my witnesses to the ends of the earth.   *ref: Acts 1:8*

I have given you the Spirit so that you too can witness that the Father has sent me as Saviour of the world.   *ref: 1 Jn 4:13-14*

And so you are my witness, my ambassador through whom God is calling others to reconciliation.   *ref: 2 Cor 5:20*

I urge you to proclaim the message, to convince, rebuke and encourage with patience.   *ref: 2 Tim 4:2*

I want you to declare what you have seen and heard, so that all may have fellowship with the Father and with me. *ref: 1 Jn 1:1-4*

The satisfaction of our real needs is almost identical with our very selfhood. Our freedom to pursue these needs is vital for our humanity to flourish. To be forced to act against one's deepest needs is an invasion of one's personhood at its very essence.

But self-deception is easy, we all need help to find our authentic needs. We get this from true friends but not from a stranger.

God is not a stranger. God is more lovingly present to us than we are to ourselves. As Paul told the Greek philosophers, 'In him we live, move and have our being.' God knows us better than we know ourselves. God loves us more deeply, more fully and more beneficially than we love ourselves. God's will is not something outside us; it is our own will at its deepest, most liberated centre.

In the depth of our being each of us has a need to be loved and to love others and so to be at peace. In second Corinthians, Paul confirms this when he says that God is 'The God of love and the God of peace.' It is for this reason that God knows what is best for us when our shallow desires and instinctual impulses might tell us otherwise. God's word, God's will, is always the word of a loving Father for our safety, for our growth, for our Godward journey and for our peace.

In his desire for their welfare, Paul exhorted the Romans, 'Let us pursue what makes for peace and mutual upbuilding.'

Now as you reflect on the words of Jesus, build up and strengthen your desire to find the peace and harmony of living in God's will,

The Will of God

My Father's will and his work were my food. May they always be yours.   *ref: Jn 4:32*

My Father's will is that in the fullness of time all things will be gathered together in me, things in heaven and things on earth.   *ref: Eph 1:9*

It was also my Father's pleasure and will that you be adopted as his child through me to the praise of his glorious grace, freely bestowed and lavished on you.   *ref: Eph 1:5-8*

Through my Spirit I reveal deeper things to you and show you what is truly human.   *ref: 1 Cor 2:10-11*

Live carefully as a wise person, filled with the Spirit, knowing my will.   *ref: Eph 5:15-18*

You can join me in asking relief: 'Father, if you are willing, remove this cup from me, yet not my will but yours be done'.   *ref: Lk 22:42*

Join me at the end of your life saying, 'I have glorified you on earth by finishing the work that you gave me to do', assured that my Father will glorify you with me in the glory I had before the world existed.   *ref: Jn 17:4-5*

The choices before us each day or each year are many and varied – to purchase a home or not to purchase, to marry or not to marry, to have another baby or not. We have to decide between good and evil behaviour, and sometimes between good and better ways of acting.

We are rarely neutral in considering what is best to do. Many reasons for acting and many reasons for not acting crowd in on us simultaneously. What gives us most pleasure and what calls for least effort is usually most attractive. To make the best decision then, we must pause and weigh up alternatives before we act. This is discernment. No one can escape this process unless he or she wishes to drift, to be pushed and pulled or to be driven by instinct.

Christians are no exception to this need for wise decision making. Everyone faces it. But as a Christian I have an extra element to help me. What does God desire me to do? Or to put it another way, how do I let God help me grow in humanness and holiness? Or to ask myself, what spirit is moving me toward each alternative? And then, what is the best way to attain my discerned goal?

Is it the Spirit of God or an evil spirit which moves me? I must first seek God's help to open my mind and to clarify my thoughts or desires before I decide. It is usually important to consult fellow believers or a spiritual guide before major decisions.

Now deeply accept God's word on the importance of openness to the divine loving will in your life.

Discernment

With spiritual wisdom and understanding, you come to know my will and grow in your knowledge of me. *ref: Col 1:9*

Only when you are spiritual can you know the gifts I bestow upon you. These are foolishness to unspiritual people. *ref: 1 Cor 2:10-15*

Walking in my will, you lead a life worthy of me, bearing fruit in every good work, and growing in your knowledge of me. *ref: Col 1:9-10*

Do not be conformed to this world. Transform and renew your mind so as to discover what is good, acceptable and perfect. *ref: Rom 12:2*

I want you to be complete in everything good, and always to do what is pleasing in my sight. *ref: Heb 13:20-21*

I invite you to continually purify your soul by obedience to my truth. *ref: 1 Pet 1:22*

My loving will for you is always your peace. *ref: 1 Cor 7:15*

Pray for your friends too. May they stand mature, fully assured in everything that I will. *ref: Col 4:14*

The Old Testament has no word for conscience but the Hebrew idea of a clean heart comes closest to it.

In the New Testament the Greek word *syneidesis*, used mostly by Paul, can be translated as conscience. It means a moral awareness of the right and wrong in what we are doing. Through our baptism into Christ we encounter God, who at once liberates and challenges our conscience. Paul said that he glories in the witness of his conscience but that the verdict on his behaviour rests finally on God's word.

Church teaching says, 'Conscience is the most secret core and sanctuary of the human person. There people are alone with God whose voice echoes in their depths.' Conscience presumes a sincere effort to find the truth. It is an instrument for detecting moral truth; it does not create it. It is one thing to have the truth on our side and another to wish to be on the side of truth.

By listening to the accumulated wisdom of the church we can help our conscience to receive and to respond accurately to the truth. It is through conscience that we find God's will for our lives. St. Thomas Aquinas calls conscience the light of God's countenance on us.

No one can be forced to act contrary to his or her conscience. While one is bound to follow one's conscience faithfully even if it is in error, one must recognise that a habit of not believing something is wrong gives it a superficial appearance of being right.

Now, prayerfully hear God speaking about the precious gift of your conscience.

Conscience

Hold fast to the mystery of faith with a clear conscience. *ref: 1 Tim 3:8*

Approach me with a true heart, in full assurance of faith, washed clean from an evil conscience, acting honourably in all things.   *ref: Heb 10:22; 13:18*

Then worship with a clear conscience and live in gratitude before me.   *ref: 2 Tim 1:3*

Always speak the truth in Christ. Your conscience will confirm it.   *ref: Rom 9:1*

Try to live your life according to my law with a clear conscience before me.   *ref: Acts 2:15, 31*

Never obey me out of fear, but because of your conscience.   *ref: Rom 13:5*

Always act with frankness and godly sincerity. The testimony of your conscience will support you.   *ref: 2 Cor 1:12*

By speaking the truth openly you will commend yourself to the conscience of others as well.   *ref: 2 Cor 4:1-2*

Even when your conscience allows something, do not hurt those whose conscience is weak.   *ref: 1 Cor 10:23–11:1*

When you live with the hope of resurrection, you will have a clear conscience towards me and all my people.   *ref: Acts 24:15-16*

Friendship grows naturally between people who feel comfortable together and who know that they care for each other. It cannot be forced. We all know what friendship is because we know who our friends are.

Aristotle spoke about two kinds of friendship, a friendship that give pleasure and a friendship of admiration for the other's goodness. He thought that only the last one was true friendship.

In the Old Testament Abraham was called a friend of God while Moses was described as God's servant.

In secular Greek, the world *phileo,* meaning to love members of one's own people, is not used much in the New Testament. It is superceded by the word *agape* which means selfless love. However, the experience of human friendship is referred to often in the New Testament. Jesus calls his apostles his friends and he himself was called 'a friend of sinners'. He called Judas his friend even in the act of betrayal. He reminded his followers that really good friends are ready to lay down their lives for one another.

In loving our friends we are like blind people tracing with tentative fingers the unseen features of the face of God.

Now prayerfully appreciate Jesus speaking to you about enjoying friendship.

Friendship

I do not call you my servant; you are my friend. I laid down my life for you.   *ref: Jn 15:12-15*

Greet your friends by name, sharing with them and welcoming them always.   *ref: Rom 16:1-16*

Remember your friends in prayer. Visit them and to share spiritual gifts. Encourage each other in faith.   *ref: Rom 1:9-13*

Pray for your friends' safety and be refreshed in their company and in my peace.   *ref: Rom 15:31-32*

Always share the good news of your blessings with your friends.   *ref: Mk 5:19*

Share your friends with others especially in times of illness. *ref: Phil 2:19-30*

Pray constantly for one another and share each other's tears in time of sorrow.   *ref: 2 Tim 1:3-4*

Even when you are betrayed, or let down by someone, try, like me, to continue saying 'My friend'.   *ref: Mt 26:50*

Welcome the visits of friends. Work hard for them. Comfort them and wrestle in prayer for them.   *ref: Col 4:10-13*

Hospitality simply means helping another to feel more welcome or less a stranger in any situation. Many people do it all the time in their family life, at work or while recreating together. It can be offered by a smile, a gesture, by giving a gift, through a word or even by listening in silence. In the contemporary world there is much loneliness even among people living together. Sadly, some people live and die with the experience of being a stranger, even within a Christian community.

The Old Testament believers were expected to be hospitable, always to welcome the stranger. God told them, 'You shall also love the stranger, for you were strangers in the land of Egypt.' In the New Testament the Greek word *xenos* is used for strangers. At the Last Judgement, Jesus himself is the *xenos* – 'I was a stranger and you made me welcome ... I was in prison and you came to see me.' Loneliness can be a real prison for many in the modern world.

When the Word of God came into the world he was not welcomed, as John reminds us, and for his birth there was no room at the inn. During his early life Jesus depended on hospitality when he stayed at the home of Simon and Andrew and when Levi invited him to accept a meal. He pointed to the Good Samaritan who gave hospitality to the injured man. We all hope that we will hear the words 'I was a stranger and you welcomed me' at the Last Judgement.

Now, reflect in prayer on Jesus' invitation to practise hospitality.

Hospitality

I washed my disciples feet. I ask you to offer similar hospitality to all.   *ref: Jn 13:1-17*

I enjoyed the hospitality of Levi and Zacchaeus.   *ref: Lk 19:1-10*

I praised the hospitality of the Samaritan to a stranger.   *ref: Lk 10:33-37*

I eagerly desired to share my last supper, my supreme act of hospitality with my apostles. I will celebrate with you again in the kingdom.   *ref: Jn 22:15*

Always enjoy the hospitality of your friends as Paul did with Simon in his home by the sea.   *ref: Philem 22*

Open your home in hospitality to church groups as did Prisca and Aquila. Paul did the same for all who came to him.   *ref: Acts 16:3-5; 28:30*

Do not neglect to visit or write to those in prison or to those being tortured as though you yourself were being tortured.   *ref: Heb 13:1-3*

Following my example, be hospitable to all without complaining.   *ref: 1 Pet 4:9*

Heaven is a wedding banquet of hospitality to which all, the good and bad, the crippled, the blind and the lame are invited.   *ref: Mt 22:1-10*

In the past, meals were mostly shared events in families. This is no longer true in the developed world where many people eat quickly, irregularly or alone. Apart from the moments of celebration when friends choose to dine out or to prepare a meal together, meals are losing their power to build friendships. Yet many Christians still celebrate the liturgy of life in family meals after Baptisms, First Communions, Confirmations, weddings and funerals.

The Bible abounds in stories of meals shared and how this togetherness can express friendship with God and with one another. The religious language of love easily becomes the language of meals shared at a common table. Jesus often ate with ordinary people, with public sinners and with those on the edge of society. Luke records the taunt of the Pharisees: 'This man welcomes sinners and eats with them.'

His feeding miracles proclaimed the magnanimity of God and were signs that the kingdom of God had arrived. Everyone was welcome at table with Jesus, even the man who had decided to betray him. His last meal summarised, enacted and symbolised his life of love and self-giving. He asked his followers to continue celebrating it: 'Do this in memory of me.' Eucharist is God's table invitation to us; it is God speaking to us. It is God offering all of himself to us before it is our offering of ourselves to God.

Now, prayerfully listen to Jesus speaking to you about the symbolism and significance of meals in his life and in yours.

Meals

The best description I could find for heaven was a banquet with God, my Father and yours.   *ref: Mt 22:2.*

During my life on earth I joined in the banquet given by Levi to celebrate with his friends.   *ref: Lk 5:29*

Although my hour had not yet come, I increased the flow of wine at a wedding feast.   *ref: Jn 2:1-11*

In my compassion for the hungry crowd I fed them with loaves and fishes.   *ref: Lk 9:12-17*

At a meal in the Pharisee's house, I received a woman's love and praised her.   *ref: Lk 7:36-50*

At Bethany I enjoyed meals in the company of my friends Martha, Mary and Lazarus.   *ref: Jn 12:1-3*

I longed to share my last meal and to make it a memorial of my covenant with you.   *ref: Lk 22:14, 15, 20*

As we broke bread together in the inn at Emmaus, I warmed the hearts of my disciples to my love.   *ref: Lk 24:28-31*

Cherish the love of friends at meals as I did when I prepared and served breakfast for my tired disciples on the beach at Tiberias.   *ref: Jn 21:12*

In the Old Testament the Hebrew word *leb*, meaning one's physical heart, was used figuratively to describe a person's deepest self, the place where courageous plans and decisions such as to trust in God's love and to love others were made.

We are told that God looked at the heart and that he called his people to love him with all their heart. We are also told that God knew the secrets of their hearts. God often asked them not to harden their hearts against divine love. His search was for hearts who love like the divine heart.

When some in Israel refused to believe in God's love and turned away to worship false gods, God appealed, 'Come back to me with all your heart.' The God of love always accepted a contrite heart and is portrayed as putting new hearts into people who were willing to change. The psalmist says that our hearts are made to trust God who always saves the upright of heart. In Zephaniah, God tells the people to rejoice and exult in divine love with all their hearts. And in very human language the Psalmist also tells us that wine gladdens our hearts.

In the New Testament, the Greek word *kardia* for heart is used as the seat of feelings, emotions, desires and decisions. It is also our religious centre which receives God's love, relishes that love and passes it on to others.

Now open your heart to God speaking to you of his loving heart, and encouraging you to live lovingly.

A Loving Heart

It is my wish that my Son dwells in your heart through faith, as you are being rooted and grounded in love.   *ref: Eph 3:17*

I have written my law of love in your heart. I am always your God and you are my people.   *ref: Heb 8:10*

My love is poured into your heart by my Holy Spirit who has been given to you.   *ref: Rom 5:5*

Always think well of your friends and hold them in your heart as Paul held his friends at Philippi. All of you share in God's grace together.   *ref: Phil 1:7*

Like Philemon and Paul, reach out to the marginalised in society by forgiving and welcoming them always.   *ref: Philem 8-21*

And refresh the hearts of others by doing favours for them as Paul asked Philemon to do for him.   *ref: Philem 8-21*

Have unity of spirit, sympathy, love for one another, a tender heart and a humble mind.   *ref: 1 Pet 3-8*

Just as you celebrate the Eucharist together in unity, enjoy your daily food together with glad and generous hearts.   *ref: Acts 2:46*

In the Old Testament the word *zakak* was used to describe something pure or flawless. The Ark of the Covenant was decorated with gold that was zakak. Moral purity, purity of the heart was expected of God's people. The Psalmist prayed 'Teach me your way O Lord, that I may walk in your truth; give me an undivided heart to revere your name'.

Jesus said that the hearts of some had grown dull. When Paul's Jewish opponents in Rome were insisting on circumcision for Gentiles, Paul said that real circumcision was a matter of the heart, spiritual not physical. The author of Hebrews appeals, 'Take care, my brothers and sisters, that none of you may have an unbelieving heart that turns away from the living God.'

In his second letter to Timothy, Paul exhorted his friend to pursue faith, love and peace, together with all those who call on the Lord from a pure heart. He assured the Philippians that the God of peace will always come into a pure heart. His beautiful prayer for them is this: 'That your love may overflow more and more with knowledge and full insight, to help you to determine what is best, so that in the day of Christ you may be pure and blameless.' Jesus invited all people to find rest in him, saying that he was gentle and humble of heart.

It is worth noting that Jesus did not campaign on issues; he called for transformation of hearts.

In Proverbs God tells us that a glad heart makes a cheerful countenance and a cheerful heart is a good medicine.

Now listen prayerfully to God's praise of a pure heart.

Purity of Heart

Blessed are you when your heart is pure for you will see me, your God.   *ref: Mt 5:8*

You can always produce good out of the store of goodness that is in your heart.   *ref: Lk 6:45*

I know the human heart, and by faith I cleanse all hearts.
ref: Acts. 15:8-9

Like good soil receiving the seed, hold the seed of my word in your heart.   *ref: Lk 8:15*

Never be foolish and slow of heart to believe the words that the prophets have spoken.   *ref: Lk 24:25*

I never want a hard or an impenitent heart.   *ref: Rom 2:5*

Like I did for Lydia, I can always open your heart to listen eagerly to my words.   *ref: Acts 16:14-15*

Pray that the eyes of your heart be enlightened so that you know the hope I have called you to and the riches of your glorious inheritance.   *ref: Eph 1:18*

I never want you to lose heart, even if your outer nature is wasting away. I renew your inner nature day by day.
ref: 2 Cor 4:16

Split Personality Disorder describes a serious illness in which one person seems to have two disconnected people within them. Most of us suffer from some disconnectedness within ourselves when our behaviour or our words do not correspond to what we truly believe. Some people lead lives of pretence much of the time. On the other hand, people of integrity are manifestly honest most of the time. Integrity of life makes for good psychological health, and spiritual health is the same. In Matthews's gospel Jesus said we can have worship that is false and prayer that is dishonest: 'These people honour me with their lips but their hearts are far from me.'

He also said that one can commit adultery in one's heart, and he pointed out that if our lives are wrapped around material possessions then our hearts will be likewise.

He tells us that feigned forgiveness is not enough; we must forgive from our hearts. When Simon the magician tried to purchase the power to heal like the apostles, Peter told him to repent so that his heart would be forgiven. In the early church when Ananias tried to deceive the community about money he had gained from the sale of land, Peter asked him why Satan had led his heart to lie to the Holy Spirit.

When people rejected Jesus' teaching he quoted the Old Testament, telling them that their hearts had grown dull like some of their ancestors.

Now open your heart as you ponder God's word and its purifying power in your daily life.

Integrity of Heart

My Son and I love you through grace. We promise to comfort your heart and strengthen it in unity of word and work.   *ref: 2 Thess 2:16-17*

I ask you not to have a divided heart but to love me with all your heart, all your soul, and all your mind.   *ref: Mt 22:37*

Take my yoke upon you and learn from me, for I am gentle and humble of heart and you will find rest for your souls.   *ref: Mt 11:29*

When you cannot understand my actions, ponder them in your heart, as Mary did.   *ref: Lk 2:50-51*

Do not let your heart be troubled. Believe in me and in my Son.   *ref: Jn 14:1-2*

When you need it, let me strengthen your heart in holiness so that you may be blameless before me at the coming of my Son.   *ref: 1 Thess 3:13*

With the eyes of your heart enlightened, you will know to what hope I have called you.   *ref: Eph 1:18*

Try to give joy and loving encouragement to the hearts of your Church leaders, so that you can refresh others through them.   *ref: Philem 7*

One must have some grounds for real hope. Hope cannot be just a desire or a dream from which we create something in the future. Abraham knew that his wife Sarah was well beyond child-bearing age; humanly speaking, he could not hope for children. The ground for his hope was a promise made to him by God that he would become the father of many nations. Paul said that Abraham had hoped against hope.

The other holy people of the Old Testament had heard what God had done for Abraham. This strengthened their hope that God would fulfil the divine promises to them. Past performance and a credible promise from a trustworthy person always give ground for reliable hope.

Writing to the Colossians, Paul says that the riches of the Christian mystery are 'Christ in you, your hope of glory'. Paul's God and our God is a God who promises and who delivers – a faithful God, and in Romans Paul asks 'If God is for us, who is against us ?' We are people of the promise. Unlike Abraham, we have seen the fulfilment of God's promise to send a Redeemer. Now, like Jesus who was tested like us in every way, we also live by faith with the hope that our struggles to lead good lives will be rewarded in heaven.

In his first letter, Peter encourages us: 'Therefore prepare your minds for action; discipline yourselves, set all your hope on the grace that Jesus Christ will bring you when he is revealed.'

Now prayerfully build up your hope as you listen to God's promises.

The Promise of Hope

Hope does not disappoint because my love has been poured into your heart through the Holy Spirit that has been given to you.   *ref: Rom 5:5*

All creation lives in hope that it will be set free from its bondage to decay and obtain the freedom of the glory of my children.   *ref: Rom 8:20*

Pray that I the God of hope will fill you with all joy and peace in believing. Then you will abound in hope by the power of the Holy Spirit.   *ref: Rom 15:13*

Your faith and love for others come from the hope laid up for you in heaven which came to you in the word of truth, the gospel. Never shift from this hope promised by the gospel.   *ref: Col 1:5, 23*

I will not overlook your work and your love in serving others. Keep showing the same diligence so as to realise the full assurance of hope to the end.   *ref: Heb 6:11-12*

You faith is the assurance of things hoped for, the conviction of things not seen.   *ref: Heb 11:1*

Hold fast to the confession of your hope without wavering, for I who have promised am faithful.   *ref: Heb 10:23*

Healing is often narrowly understood as removing physical illness or injury. However, some illnesses can be a symptom of a deeper need for healing. Illness occurs when any aspect of our personhood – body, mind or spirit – is not functioning well or when its unity fragments. When all parts of our bodies are functioning and co-ordinating well, the healing of an injury or illness is facilitated.

No matter how healthy our bodies may be, we still need healthy minds to think clearly and hearts that are at peace. Very often, people whose bodies are not functioning well because of age or injury have much more peace of heart than those who are physically well.

Our own addictions, selfishness, fear, anxiety, guilt, resentment, lack of forgiveness are all sources of illness. However, our deepest illness is feeling unloved by God. Feeling unloved by others can also be a source of illness. Being without a reason to live or a reason to die amounts to another deep need for healing.

Every group of believers is ideally a healing community where each one is actively concerned about the total health of the others. We know that God has given some individuals a special gift for healing. And God's answer to our prayers for healing is often the strength to heal ourselves.

Mark tells us about the anointing of the sick by the apostles, and James tells us that this was done by the presbyters. Until the fourth century, blessed oil was taken home and applied by lay people to bring healing.

Now in your prayer, reflect on God's word about the deeper meaning of healing.

Healing

During my earthly life I healed many who were sick with various diseases.   *ref: Mk 1:34*

My deepest healing took place when I said, 'Peace I leave with you; my peace I give you, a peace the world cannot give'. Accept this gift.   *ref: Jn 14:27*

I offer you profound healing when I say to you, 'Do not let your hearts be troubled and do not let them be afraid'. *ref: Jn 14:27*

I still wish to open eyes and ears that need healing so that they may see and hear me.   *ref: Mt 13:15-16*

Let me heal the paralysis of any unforgiveness which may reside in your heart.   *ref: Lk 9:2-8*

Confess your sins to one another and pray for one another, so that you may be healed.   *ref: Jas 5:16*

I healed the leper by my compassionate touch. Your loving touch has power to heal too.   *ref: Mk 1:40-41*

Your prayer to me for the healing of friends is very powerful.   *ref: Lk 7:2-10*

I invite you to heal even your enemies, by a loving touch as I did in Gethemene.   *ref: Lk 22:50-51*

Hear my words as I send you out to proclaim my kingdom and to heal.   *ref: Lk 9:1-2*

All human living involves some struggle, but with hope that the future will be better than the present we are sustained in those struggles.

In ancient Greece the Stoics thought that there were no reasons to hope; their message was one of enduring what will never change. The ancient faith of Buddhism preaches that happiness consists in getting rid of all desires in the hope of reaching happiness on earth.

While God's people were exiles in Egypt they yearned in hope to reach the Promised Land. Some gave up and some persevered, depending on their confidence in God's promises. However it was only in later times that a clearer hope for life after death emerged for them.

In the New Testament the Christians are portrayed as people of hope in spite of personal struggle and severe persecution. Writing to the Romans, Paul said that he boasted of his sufferings because they produced endurance which produced character. This he said, led to hope and this hope was founded on the resurrection of Christ. He assured them that the hope offered does not disappooint us because the Holy Spirit has poured God's love into our hearts. Christian hope and its struggles are based on our faith and our trust in a loving God who vindicated Jesus' faith and trust by his resurrection.

This hope has sustained believers to work courageously in the fields of education, medicine, social justice and political progress throughout the history of the church, and it continues to do so today. Pope Benedict XVI writes: 'All serious and upright human conduct is hope in action.'

Here are God's words promising you the hope that will sustain you on your journey.

The Struggle of Hope

I ask you to remain steadfast in trials. Receive encouragement from my scriptures. In this way you will continue in hope. *ref: Rom 15:4*

As you toil and struggle, set your hope on me who saves all people, especially those who believe. *ref: 1 Tim 4:10*

In hope I have saved you, but hope that is seen is not hope. You hope for what you do not see. Wait for it with patience. *ref: Rom 8:24-25*

Rejoice in hope, be patient in suffering, persevere in prayer. *ref: Rom 12:12*

Let no trials discourage or remove your hope in the resurrection of the dead. *ref: Acts 23:6*

I remind you that endurance produces character, character that produces hope, a hope that does not disappoint. *ref: Rom 5:3-5*

Always be ready to make your defence, giving an account for the hope that is in you. Yet do it with gentleness and reverence. *ref: 1 Pet 3:15*

Continue to live a life that is self-controlled, upright and godly while you wait for the blessed hope and manifestation of my glory. *ref: Tit 2:12-13*

WEEK THREE

This sacred synod earnestly and specifically urges all the
Christian faithful …
to learn by frequent reading of the scriptures
the excelling knowledge of Jesus Christ.
As St Jerome stresses:
'Ignorance of the scriptures is ignorance of Christ.'
And let the faithful remember that prayer should
accompany the reading of the sacred scriptures,
so that God and we may talk together.

Vatican Council II, *Divine Revelation*, 25

St Thomas Aquinas wrote: 'We do not know what God is' and St Augustine said that if we could understand God, God would not be God. God as God is incomprehensible and can never be known in the ordinary sense of the word *known*.

While each of us needs our present image of God to sustain us, we also need to gradually let go of this partial idol-image. Then we will be more open to receive God who continues to reveal the divine more fully to us. For instance, to think or to speak about God only as male is a limiting experience. We need to constantly review many of our recited prayers and hymns, so that we can come to know God more truly.

Science answers many of the questions to which we attributed the direct action of God in the past. The vastness of the universe with over 400 billion galaxies, questions our limited images of God's creative work. Using God to fill the gaps in our knowledge could lead to a gradual lessening of faith if science eventually fills those gaps. Karl Rahner speaks of 'a bleaker spirituality' for thinking people in the future. Others describe it as entering into a collective dark night of the soul or into a contemplative silence before God.

Our first response to God can only be one of awe and wonder, as we bow in adoration before the infinite incomprehensibility of the divine. It is only after this act of worship before God's supremacy, that we can praise and celebrate God's personal love for us in Jesus.

Now, in a spirit of profound reverence, pray the words, 'Speak Lord, I am listening.'

The Supremacy of God

No idol in the world really exists. There is no God but me.
Through me are all things and through me all things exist.
ref: 1 Cor 8:4-6

The depth of my wisdom, of my knowledge and of my
judgements are unsearchable. How inscrutable my ways.
ref: Rom 11:33

From me, and through me, and to me, are all things. Mine
is the glory forever.   *ref: Rom 11:34-36*

I am the only Sovereign, the King of kings and the Lord of
lords. I alone have immortality and I dwell in unapproachable light. No one has ever seen me or can see me. To me
is due honour and eternal dominion.   *ref: 1 Tim 6:15-16*

I, the Lord of heaven and earth made the world and everything in it. I do not live in shrines made by human hands.
Nor am I served by human hands. I give to all mortals life
and breath and all things.   *ref: Acts 17:24-25*

No one is good but me alone.   *ref: Lk 18:19*

I am spirit and those who worship me worthily, do so in
spirit and in truth.   *ref: Jn 4:24*

In me, you live, move and have your being.   *ref: Acts 17:28*

One meaning of the Hebrew word *kabod,* used for glory, is something heavy or weighty. It is also used to describe someone who was impressive or worthy.

In the Old Testament God is glorious, and any manifestation of God, such as his people and his victory over the Pharaoh, is a revelation of his glory. No one could look directly on God's glory; it was always behind a cloud.

Strictly speaking we cannot give glory to God; we can only recognise God's glory, celebrate it and encourage others to find it in their lives. God manifests the divine glory through our goodness; we can be messengers and manifestations of this glory.

The New Testament uses the Greek word *doxa* for glory. Jesus is the supreme manifestation of God's glory. At the Last Supper he told us that through faith we already share in that glory. All mere human glory, like status or fame, will pass away. In the words of St Ireneus, 'The glory of God is the human person fully alive, and when fully alive, the human person is the manifestation of God.' Nature also manifests God's glory:

Earth is crammed with heaven

and every bush afire with God

But only those who see take off their shoes.

The rest sit round and pick blackberries.

(Elizabeth Browning)

De Chardin said that the world is 'a diaphony of the divine'.

Now, let God speak to you about the divine glory, the glory of Christ and about your own glory which reflects this.

The Glory of God

To me, your God, belongs glory and power for ever and ever.   *ref: 1 Pet 4:11*

I encourage you to join my angels in prayer. Pray 'Glory to God in the highest.'   *ref: Lk 2:13*

I gave glory to my Son that he might return glory to me. *ref: Jn 17:5*

Like my Son Jesus, I ask you to have the desire to glorify my name and to live for its glory.   *ref: Jn 12:27-28*

When he healed the paralytic the people were filled with awe and glorified me.   *ref: Mt 9:8*

The return of Lazarus to life gave glory to my Son and to me.   *ref: Jn 11:4*

By your baptism you were buried with him into death. Just as he was raised by my glory, so you now can walk in newness of life.   *ref: Rom 6:3-4*

It is true that you fall short of my glory, but you are justified by the gift of my grace.   *ref: Rom 3:23-25*

What is sown in weakness will be raised in glory. With your resurrection, what is raised will be imperishable.   *ref: 1 Cor 15:42-43*

In the new Jerusalem, the city will have no need for sun or moon to shine on it, for my glory is its light.   *ref: Rev 2:22-23*

The word covenant means a solemn pledge or promise. It is used about seventy times in the Old Testament. The Jewish people were chosen by God with a promise to care for them in a special way. This has not changed. God brought Abraham out of Ur, freed the Israelites from Egypt, brought them safely through the desert and gave them the promised land. God promised love and remained faithful to those promises despite some of the people's infidelity. This was the first covenant, to which God was always faithful.

A traditional title for the New Testament is the Second or New Covenant. The new covenant is the fulfilment of the old. The word covenant is used thirty three times in the New Testament. Jesus called the wine at the Last Supper the new covenant in his blood. Paul stresses its unconditional validity in Christ who manifests and mediates God's loving irreversible decision, a divine faithful relationship with us. It expresses God's saving purpose first given to the Jewish people and now given to Christians also.

There are three deep human experiences: to be chosen in love, to be given a responsibility and to be trusted. These experiences, which God offers each one of us, inspire us and fill us with a deep sense of self-worth and a desire to live up to it. God's covenant is a personal promise and a call.

Now prayerfully take God's uplifting words into your heart.

The Fidelity of God

I chose you before the foundation of the world, to be holy and blameless before me in love. *ref: Eph 1:3-4.*

I made a covenant with you through the house of Israel when I wrote my law into their hearts. *ref: Heb 8:10*

I made my covenant with you in my chosen people. My gifts and my calling are irrevocable. *ref: Rom 11:27-29*

I renewed my choice of you in Abraham and then in my Son, Jesus. *ref: Gal 3:16*

My Son is my irrevocable 'yes' to you for I am faithful. For my Son it was never 'yes' and 'no'. In him every one of my promises is a 'yes'. *ref: 2 Cor 1:19-20*

He is the mediator of the new everlasting covenant, so that you may receive the promised eternal inheritance. He now appears in my presence on your behalf. *ref: Heb 9:15, 24*

Since you have my faithful promises, cleanse yourself of every defilement of body and spirit. *ref: 2 Cor 7:1*

But no infidelity on your part can nullify my faithfulness. *ref: Rom 3:3*

Such is the confidence you have through Christ in me that you are now competent to be a minister of this new covenant to others. *ref: 2 Cor 3:4-6*

In the Old Testament, God alone has life. God is the Lord of all life and so, human life is simply God's gift. Obedience to the Law and to Wisdom would bring God's people a long and happy life but death ended life. It did not fulfil it.

In the New Testament, John tells us that Jesus came so that we might have life abundantly. Here John is talking about life of a different quality, the life of God. John says that Christ has this God-life in himself. Christ is life itself. When Jesus died on the cross he gave up his human life which John calls *psyche* but his real life *zoe* lives on. Christ gives this life to believers. Jesus is described by John as the bread of life, the water of life, the light of life, and his words are life.

This new life gives us the power to experience God's love and the power to pass it on to others. God assures us that this new life-in-abundance gives us the confidence to drive out all fear and to live with a deep joy.

John said that his purpose in writing his gospel was that the readers might come to believe that Jesus is the Messiah, the Son of God, and that through believing they may have life in his name.

In his first letter, John shows how to measure the quality of this God-life in us: 'We have passed over from death to life because we love one another. Whoever does not love, abides in death.'

Now prayerfully meditate on your unspeakable privilege of sharing the life of God.

New Life in Christ

Eternal life is knowing me the only true God and my Son Jesus Christ whom I sent.   *ref: Jn 17:3*

I so loved you that I gave you my only Son, that when you believe in him you may not perish but may have eternal life.   *ref: Jn 3:15*

My Son was lifted up on the cross so that believing in him you have eternal life . *ref: Jn 3:15*

He came that you may have life and have it abundantly. *ref: Jn 10:10*

In him, life came into being, and that life is the light of all people.   *ref: Jn 1:3-4*

He is the way for your eyes to see, the truth for your ears to hear, and the life that you can live.   *ref: Jn 14:6*

Just as I raise the dead and give them life, so also my Son gives life to you.   *ref: Jn 5:21*

Hearing my Son's word and believing in me, you have eternal life. You have passed from death to life.   *ref: Jn 5:24*

He is the resurrection and the life. Because you believe in him you will never die.   *ref: Jn 11:25*

The love and availability of Jesus for his Father and for others were expressions of his deep freedom. He was fully human but he was free of self-pity and free from the demands of self-comfort.

He was equally free in dealing with priests, publicans, lawyers, lepers, tax collectors, foreign women, Roman legionaries, arrogant politicians, abused prostitutes, anxious parents and little children. Public opinion did not influence him. Nor did resentment or revenge have any place in his experience. He was a free man, always free to act lovingly.

He was free to refuse earthly kingship. He did not return violence for violence used against him. He remained free to follow his mission even though his family thought he was insane and even when some disciples did not believe him.

He was free from literal obedience to law and tradition. while respecting both. He was free to set aside Sabbath observance and to challenge capital punishment for a woman caught in adultery. Threats from the authorities were ineffectual against him. As a travelling preacher he was free of property ownership and of possessions.

Although he felt massive fear in the face of death, and overwhelming sadness after betrayal, he freely chose to overcome these for the sake of his mission. In the end he was crucified for what he did but as John records his words, 'I lay down my life in order to take it up again. No one takes it from me.' Jesus was free to let go of life itself.

Now prayerfully accept Jesus' invitation to experience the same freedom in your life.

The Freedom of Christ

I did not respond to violence with violence. You have the same freedom.   *ref: Mt 26:51, 52, 57*

Nor did the slavery of resentment have a place in my life. It need have none in yours.   *ref: Mt 26:49-50*

The letter of the law did not bind me. You too are free of this slavery.   *ref: Mk 2:23-28*

I was free from possessive relationships. You too have this freedom if you choose.   *ref: Jn 6:66-67*

Human respect did not enslave me. You also have this freedom.   *ref: Lk 19:7*

Racism or sexism never marred my ministry. You need never let these destroy your freedom either.   *ref: Jn 4:9, 27*

I was hungry but not a slave to food. Freedom to fast is also my gift to you.   *ref: Lk 4:1-4*

My Father's work was my reason to live, but I freely found time for rest.   *ref: Mk 6:31*

No one took my life from me. I laid it down of my own accord. I invite you to the same freedom.   *ref: Jn 10:18*

In Palestine, at the time of Jesus, sheep depended entirely on their shepherd to find pasture and water as well as protection from wolves. Psalm twenty three describes the relationship between the shepherd and his sheep. In the Old Testament, God is the shepherd of Israel who walks ahead and provides for the flock. God patiently led them out of Egypt. David was called a faithful shepherd. In Ezekiel, God tells the leaders that they had become irresponsible shepherds, feeding themselves rather than the sheep. God said that he would become their shepherd and that finally he would appoint another shepherd like David. This is Jesus. Although the shepherds were well known in the Old Testament, the thought of the shepherd laying down his life for his sheep is new.

Jesus compared God to a shepherd rejoicing when a lost sheep was found. To describe his own mission he uses the image of a shepherd who cares for, guides and is ready to die for his flock. He said that his shepherding extended beyond Israel in his desire to have one flock and one shepherd. Mark records Jesus saying that when he came to the people of Israel they were like neglected sheep, because their leaders were failing them.

In John's gospel, Jesus assures us that he, the good shepherd, knows each of us by name and that we know his voice.

He will lead us to rich pasture because he came that we might have life abundantly.

Now, prayerfully relish the personal words of the Good Shepherd to you.

The Good Shepherd

My Father sent me to become the ruler who is to shepherd his people Israel.   *ref: Mt 26*

I became the great shepherd of the sheep by my blood of the eternal covenant.   *ref: Heb 13:20*

I am the good shepherd who laid down his life for his sheep.   *ref: Jn 10:11*

Just as the Father knows me and I know the Father, I know you and you know me.   *ref: Jn 10:15*

I know you by name and you know my voice. Do not follow a stranger.   *ref: Jn 10:3-5*

I want everyone to hear my voice so that there will be one flock and one shepherd.   *ref: Jn 1:16*

I have compassion for the sheep whose shepherds neglect them. They are harassed and helpless. Pray for more labourers in the harvest.   *ref: Mt 9:36-38*

On your journey, recall that you are sent by me, even if you feel like a sheep among wolves.   *ref: Mt 10:16*

And when you suffer for doing what is right, recall that I too was led to the slaughter.   *ref: Acts 8:32*

Be an example to all because when I, the chief Shepherd, come again you will receive the crown of glory.
ref: 1 Pet 5:3-4

God breathed the breath of life into Adam. Paul speaks about the second Adam, Jesus Christ, the author of a new humanity.

In his second letter to the Corinthians, we read of a new creation. Paul says, 'If anyone is in Christ, there is a new creation; everything old has passed away.' In the same letter he writes, 'We are always carrying in the body the death of Jesus, so that the life of Jesus may also be made visible in our bodies.' And at the end of this letter Paul asks if we are 'living in the faith'. 'Test yourselves', he says, 'Do you not realise that Jesus Christ is living in you?'

Describing his own life to the Galatians, he says, 'I have been crucified with Christ; and it is no longer I who live, but Christ who lives in me. And the life I now live in the flesh I live by faith in the Son of God who loved me and gave himself for me.' And to the Philippians he writes, 'For me living is Christ and dying is gain.' He advised the Colossians, 'Since you have been raised with Christ, seek the things that are above … for you have died, and your life is hidden with Christ in God.'

There is a future fulfilment, but Paul describes the divine life as already within us. He is telling us that the Christian experience is not just following, imitating or obeying Jesus Christ. It is 'Christ who is your life' living in us now.

Think also of the many who suffer in other countries because they are Christians, and pray for them.

Now, prayerfully ponder on the gift and the challenge of living and walking in Christ.

Living the New Life

You were baptised into my Son's death and resurrection. I invite and enable you to walk in this new life.   *ref: Rom 6:1-4*

Through baptism you have been buried with Christ in his death. In his resurrection, walk now with him in newness of life.   *ref: Rom 6:4*

The wages of sin is death, but my free gift is eternal life in my Son Christ Jesus your Lord.   *ref: Rom 6:23*

If you sow to your own flesh you will reap corruption from the flesh, but if you sow to the Spirit, you will reap eternal life from the Spirit.   *ref: Gal 6:8*

In my Spirit whom I poured out richly on you through my Son your Saviour, you have become an heir according to the hope of eternal life.   *ref: Tit 3:6-7*

You claim this new life when you live by faith.   *ref: Rom 1:17*

Fight the good fight of faith. Take hold of the eternal life to which I call you.   *ref: 1 Tim 6:12*

Set your mind on things that are above, not on things that are on earth, for your life has been hidden with Christ in God. One day you will be revealed with him in glory.   *ref: Cor 3:2-3*

The Greek word *eucharistos* was used to describe something pleasant or graceful. It also meant to show a favour which usually evoked an expression of gratitude. The Greeks held gratitude in high esteem. It was applied to their gods and to worthy rulers.

Paul used different forms of the word *eucharistia* meaning thanksgiving. When he reminded the first Christians about the Eucharist, he used it at the blessing of the bread. He also used it for the gratitude we owe our God. When he received alms from the Corinthian community he wrote to them saying, 'You will be enriched in every way for your great generosity, which will produce thanksgiving to God through us.' He told the Philippians to thank God, even while they were making their petitions. And he told them that prayer, petition and an attitude of thanksgiving would cure excessive anxiety.

Some of the Corinthian Christians were given to excessive fasting and to avoiding certain foods. Paul told them that all food was good and that it should be received with a prayer of thanksgiving.

Similarly, when writing to Timothy he said that we should give thanks even while asking.

In his first letter to the Thessalonians he writes, 'Give thanks in all circumstances; for this is the will of God in Christ Jesus for you.' The author of Ephesians told the readers to sing songs of thanksgiving 'at all times and for everything in the name of our Lord Jesus Christ'.

Now, prayerfully allow God's word, spoken through Paul, awaken a new depth of gratitude in you.

Thanksgiving

You have received Christ Jesus my Son as your Lord. Continue to live your life in him, rooted and built up in him, abounding in thanksgiving.   *ref: Col 2:6-7*

I am near you. Do not worry about anything. Always pray with thanksgiving. Then my peace which surpasses all understanding will guard your heart and you mind in Christ Jesus, my Son.   *ref: Phil 4:5-7*

I am able to provide you with every blessing in abundance so that you will always have enough of everything. Be generous then and this will produce an overflow of thanksgiving to me.   *ref: 2 Cor 9:8-12*

Thank me also for the encouragement you receive through other people's faith, as you build up their faith in turn. *ref: 1 Thess 3:7-10*

Be grateful for the grace received by your friends, for the many ways in which I have enriched them.   *ref: 1 Cor 1:4-8*

Everything I have created is good; nothing to be rejected when it is received with thanksgiving, for all is sanctified by my word and by prayer.   *ref: 1 Tim 4:3-5*

In the Hebrew Bible, praise and thanks are often synonymous. In the Psalms, thanksgiving is a spontaneous expression of admiration and joy at the very thought of God. Expressions of sadness are also accompanied with thanks and praise because of the believer's trust in God. Paul states that any sincere person can admire creation and so be grateful to God the creator.

The person who has the spirit of gratitude can never be unhappy for long, since everything is received as gift. After the word 'Mammy' and 'Daddy' are expressed with feelings of love and security, the most important words a child can learn are 'please' and 'thank you'. The sentiments or feelings which will fill these words when they are understood, will greatly influence the child's capacity for living with others as an adult.

G. K. Chesterton wrote, 'The test of all happiness is gratitude. Children are grateful when Santa Claus puts gifts into their stocking, gifts of toys or sweets. Should I not be grateful then to Santa Claus when he puts in my stocking the gift of two miraculous legs? We thank people for birthday presents. Can I thank no one for the birthday present of birth itself?' Our faith enables us and calls us to live lives 'abounding in thanksgiving', as Paul recommends to the Colossians.

Gratitude does not always follow happiness, but happiness follows gratitude. Ideally, we are not grateful because we are happy; rather we are happy because we are grateful.

Now open you heart to accept God's words to you about this rich source of happiness.

Thanksgiving

Rejoice always; pray without ceasing. Give thanks in all circumstances, for this is my will in my Son for you. *ref:1 Thess 5:18*

Give thanks for everything in his name.   *ref: Eph 5:18-20*

Thank me your God who in Christ spreads in every place the fragrance that comes from knowing me. You are the aroma of Christ to me.   *ref: 2 Cor 2:14-16*

Continue to live your life in my Son, rooted and built up in him, abounding in thanksgiving . *ref: Col 2:6-7*

I created all food to be received with thanksgiving. *ref 1 Tim 4:3*

Whether you eat or abstain, do so in my honour and always give thanks.   *ref: Rom 14:6*

Lest you forget to thank others for favours given you, recall the disappointment of my Son when only one leper returned with gratitude.   *ref: Lk 17:16*

I invite you to join the angels before my throne singing: 'Blessing and glory, wisdom and thanksgiving, honour and power and might be to our God forever and ever, Amen.' *ref: Rev 7:11-12*

The Old and New Testaments speak of many who suffered and died because they practised their faith in worship or in love for others. We read in the Acts of the Apostles that Paul's sufferings were foretold by God to Ananias, 'I myself will show him how much he must suffer for the sake of my name.' This prediction was vividly fulfilled in Paul's life right up to his beheading in Rome. He is a model for all of us when we have to suffer in living out our faith in a life of active love for others.

Paul told the Corinthian community that 'To the present hour we are hungry and thirsty, poorly clothed, beaten, homeless and we grow weary from the work of our own hands.' He also reminded them that he was reviled, persecuted and slandered. He described how his suffering made him feel like 'the rubbish of the world, the dregs of all things'.

However, his greatest suffering came from his unsatisfied desire to see Christ fully alive in all whom he met. He called the Galatians 'my children for whom I am again in the pain of childbirth until Christ is formed in you.' There were some of his own communities, as in Philippi, who made him suffer because of envy and rivalry.

Each of us will suffer in our efforts to let Christ live in us again and from our desire to love as he does.

Now reflect on the meaning, the value and the inevitability of Christian suffering as Jesus continues to live and love through you.

Suffering for Christ

If you suffer for the name of my Son, you are blessed and the spirit of glory which is my Spirit is resting on you. You glorify me because you bear my name.   *ref: 1 Pet 4:14-16*

Even if you suffer for doing what is right, you are blessed because you sanctify my Son Jesus as Lord in your heart. *ref: 1 Pet 3:13-15*

I am giving you the privilege of not only believing in him, but of suffering for him as well.   *ref: Phil 1:29*

Because of the surpassing value of knowing my Son, you can regard everything else as loss.   *ref: Phil 3:7-9*

Just as the sufferings of my Son are abundant for you, so too is my consolation abundant through him.   *ref: 2 Cor 1:3-5*

You suffer for the gospel with many others around the world. In doing this you can rely on my power too. *ref: 2 Tim 1:8*

Suffering produces endurance which produces character. Character produces hope which does not disappoint you because my love has been poured into your heart through the Holy Spirit.   *ref: Rom 5:3-5*

Suffering of some kind is part of being human. Good and evil people, religious and non-religious people all suffer.

There are different origins for suffering. Our genetic history and our past life experiences can cause suffering for us many years later. Scientists work to prevent this but in the meantime we live with no complete solution.

We can cause suffering to the next generation by polluting the atmosphere now. When parents fail to love their children unconditionally, they cause future suffering in their lives. We can only try to lessen these and pray for endurance and healing.

Sometimes we cause our own suffering when we take drugs, eat or drink too much or too little, consume unhealthy food, work too hard, take no exercise or drive our cars carelessly. We can alleviate these sufferings by acting more wisely, by seeking medical help and by praying for healing.

In the Old Testament, suffering was sometimes seen as God's punishment or simply as God testing his friends as in the case of Job.

Real Christian suffering is different. It is suffering which results from leading a Christ-like life. To keep on loving when it is not returned or when it is painful brings suffering. Through our identity with Jesus in our baptism, he now lives, loves and suffers in us. In a deep way, his earthly sufferings are not complete; they continue in us as we live our Christian lives. In our Christian sufferings we are not merely suffering *for* Jesus; we are suffering *with* him.

Now listen prayerfully to Jesus' words through Peter, as they encourage you in suffering because of your faith.

Suffering with Christ

Rejoice when you suffer for the welfare of others. You are making up what is lacking in my afflictions for the sake of my body the church.   *ref: Col 1:24*

I want you to know me and the power of my resurrection, sharing in my sufferings by becoming like me in death. In this way, you too will attain the resurrection from the dead. *ref: Phil 3:10-11*

You are God's child, my co-heir, a joint heir with me. You suffer with me; you will also be glorified with me.   *ref: Rom 8:17*

I suffered for you, leaving you an example so that you could follow in my steps. I was abused but did not threaten, entrusting myself to God. By my wounds you have been healed.   *ref: 1 Pet 2:22-24*

Rejoice in so far as you share my suffering, so that you may be glad and shout for joy. You will rejoice when my glory is revealed.   *ref: 1 Pet 4:13*

When you have suffered for a little while, my Father, the God of all grace will restore, support, strengthen and establish you.   *ref: 1 Pet 5:10*

Reach out to share the suffering of others because together you are my Son's body.   *ref: 1 Cor 12:26*

To stay alive, to be successful and especially to build friendships, we need to persevere and to endure in spite of difficulties along the way.

In the Old Testament, the frequently used Greek word *hypomeno* means to endure patiently and to persevere in overcoming difficulties, while living out any aspect of our friendship with God. We are all tempted to give up at times.

In the New Testament, we are assured that God's word and the new covenant endure despite human failures. God's gifts of faith, hope and love to us also endure. In response the believer is encouraged to persevere in patient but active waiting sustained by hope. As people of faith we receive an inner strength that enables us to hold up under doubt or stress. It is God who gives the virtue of endurance.

In his letters to Timothy, Paul states that believers persevere in faith, love, holiness and in what they have learned and believed. In John's gospel, this becomes perseverance with living in Christ. The letter to the Hebrews lays great stress on endurance in time of discouragement and persecution.

The scripture tells us that true believers have faith in God's love and in his plan, and consequently that they will endure; they will not be overcome. They remain committed to leading a good life despite discouraging difficulties. Trials strengthen faith. For those who endure, the final things are already possessed, although not yet fully experienced.

Now open your heart prayerfully to God's encouraging words to you on your life journey.

Endurance

My Son Jesus is the pioneer and the one who perfects your faith. He endured the suffering and rejection of the cross in spite of its shame.   *ref: Heb 12:2-4*

Reflecting on the hardships and suffering of my Son, you will endure with him and you will reign with him.   *ref: 2 Tim 2:8-12*

Try to endure especially what will further the salvation of others.   *ref: 2. Tim 2:10*

When you accept the seed of my word deeply you too will endure if trials come just as my Son did.   *ref: Mt 13:21*

I am faithful to you. You will never be tested without my strength enabling you to endure.   *ref: 1 Cor 10:13*

Blessed are you when you endure temptation. You will have stood the test and will receive the crown of life that I have promised to those who love me.   *ref: Jas 1:12*

True love bears all things, believes all things, hopes all things and endures all things.   *ref: 1 Cor 13:7*

My word endures forever. That word is the good news announced by my Son.   *ref: 1 Pet 1:25*

Up until the time of Jesus many thought that wealth and possessions were a sign of God's favour and the reward for a good life. This view also underlies the big question that poor people have about their shortage of basic necessities. We know that this is not caused by God but by the excessive wealth of others and by systems which protect it.

God wants everyone to have enough, to enjoy it and to share with those in need. God does not want poverty but asks that we share what we have. Jesus taught clearly that it is the believer's attitude towards wealth that matters. He said that we cannot love God and money. Money here means more than wealth; it means the acquisitive instinct.

Storing wealth which we do not need is wrong. The rich man who denied Lazarus his crumbs was clearly condemned, and Jesus called the honest hard-working rich man a fool because he continued to amass wealth. Detachment from wealth is a prerequisite for discipleship. Food for myself and my family could be described as a material problem for me, but food for others is a spiritual one for me. Jesus warns that the seed of God's word can be choked by the lure of wealth. Unshared wealth can rivet us to this life. In his first letter John states, 'If anyone is well off in worldly possessions and sees his brother in need but closes his heart to him, how can the love of God remain in him?' What I do not need is not mine.

Listen to Jesus saying to you as you pray, 'If anyone has ears to hear, let them listen.'

Possessions

Do not store up treasures on earth lest your heart also be there. Strive first for my kingdom and righteousness. All you need will be given to you.   *ref: Mt 6:19, 33*

You cannot serve me and serve money. You cannot be devoted to me and to wealth.   *ref: Lk 16:13*

Your life is not the abundance of possessions. Be on your guard against all kinds of greed.   *ref: Lk 12:15*

One can have an outward show of godliness and yet be a lover of money and not love me.   *ref: 2 Tim 3:2 and Heb 13:5*

Those who want to be rich are tempted and trapped by desires leading to destruction. Eagerness to be rich can lead to loss of faith.   *ref: 1 Tim 6:9-10*

The seed of my word can be choked to fruitlessness by the lure of wealth and possessions.   *ref: Mt 13:22*

No worthy office-holder in my church can be a lover of money.   *ref: 1 Tim 3:1-3*

How can my love abide in you if you have the world's goods and refuse to help those in need?   *ref: 1 Jn 3:17*

How hard it is for those who have wealth to enter my kingdom.   *ref: Lk 18:24*

In the Old Testament, Abraham is the great model of detachment. He left his country and offered to sacrifice his son.

Jesus enjoyed the good things of life like friendship, food, wine and a cushion under his head, but he lived a non-possessive simple life. In total trust and fidelity to the call of his Father and in love of others, he was detached from family, from friends, and from material things. In his letter to the Philippians, Paul reminds us that Jesus was detached even from the privileges of his divinity.

When our treasures do not possess us we are free to let them go. Detachment enables us to choose freely rather than to act out of fear, compulsion, or routine. Detachment is a virtue that allows us to choose what most fulfils our deepest ideals or values, rather than being enslaved to our instinctual urges.

God gifts us with friends and with a beautiful world for our enjoyment. Our willingness to share them in a selfless way is a measure of our detachment from them. Our faith tells us that detachment by self-control, for self-giving and for generous availability to others is part of discipleship. Jesus said that we cannot love God and mammon at the same time. Mammon is usually translated as wealth but more deeply it means greed. Money or material possessions must never become an absolute priority in our Christian lives.

Now, prayerfully hear Jesus inviting you to grow in detachment and to live simply so that others may simply live.

Detachment

I was rich in my divinity but for your sake I became poor so that by my poverty you might become rich. *ref: 2 Cor 8:9*

I was born in the simplicity of a stable and I earned my living as a village carpenter. *ref: Lk 2:12 and Mk 63*

Foxes have holes and birds of the air have nests but for three years I had nowhere to lay my head. *ref: Mt 8:20*

Be on your guard against all kinds of greed; your life does not consist in the abundance of possessions. *ref: Lk 12:15*

And I ask you to share, but not under compulsion. My Father loves a cheerful giver. *ref: 2 Cor 2:7*

The poor you will always have with you, and they are blessed. Show them kindness when you can, and share your resources with them. *ref: Lk 6:20, Mk 14:7, Rom 15:25-27*

Try to be content with essential food and clothing. If you are attached to riches, you can be trapped by senseless desires. *ref: 1 Tim 6:8-10*

One day your life will come to an end. If you store up treasures for yourself ask whose will they become? Aim rather to become rich toward me. *ref: Lk 12:20-21*

Worship and prayer are important, but they are acceptable to God only when we share our lives with others. Sharing authenticates prayer. Towards the end of Matthews's gospel Jesus describes a scene when each of us will be judged finally on how we shared. Jesus rewards those who shared their food with the hungry, their clothes with the naked, their time with prisoners and strangers.

People need basics like food, drink and clothing but their real needs go deeper. Many are hungry for friendship, for someone to spend time with them. People need our listening ear, our friendly words, our patience, our forgiveness, our kind deeds and our time. When people suffer they need our willingness to share their pain. This level of sharing is more demanding than sharing money and possessions.

God asks us to share first of all with those who live with us, then with those whom we meet, and finally to reach out in love for all. Can we hear the voice of the voiceless, the silent cry of the person beside us whose selfishness or aggressive behaviour covers the greatest poverty of all – the loneliness of not being loved?.

Our motives for sharing are usually mixed; there is no such a thing as perfect purity of intention. However, where there is sharing, God is in it. The quality of our sharing is an accurate measure of our love.

Now, prayerfully meditate on God's call and on God's power within you, to share.

Sharing with Others

The cup of blessing which you bless is a sharing in the blood of my Son. The bread you break is a sharing in his body.   *ref: 1 Cor 10:16*

Continue to share yourself with me first of all. Then you will know the privilege of sharing, even beyond your means, with others in their need.   *ref: 2 Cor 8:3-5*

Labour and work honestly, so that you will have something to share with the needy.   *ref: Eph 4:28*

Do not neglect to do good and to share what you have, for such sacrifices are pleasing to me.   *ref: Heb 13:16*

Do not set your hopes on the uncertainty of riches. You must do good and be rich in good works, generous and ready to share.   *ref: 1 Tim 6:17-18*

If you have abundance, share with those in need.   *ref: Lk 3:11*

You glorify me when you confess the gospel and when you share generously with others.   *ref 2 Cor 9:13*

Give thanks to me your Father who has enabled you to share in the inheritance of the saints in the light.   *ref: Col 1:12*

One dictionary definition of family is a group of people related by blood or marriage. Many of us came from a family with grandparents, parents and siblings with whom we were close. Some were less fortunate in having had disruption of some kind in the family relationships.

The traditional understanding of family should be considered ideal, but it is becoming less frequent. There are single parent families as there always were because of a parent's death, but these are increasing for many other reasons. There are many childless couples who are loving family units.

While still keeping the ideal in mind, some look more widely at what group of individuals might constitute a family. In practice today, a family is not necessarily made up of a father, mother and children enveloped in love and permanency. As Christians we can describe and have our opinion about what is ideal, but Jesus told us, 'Do not judge and you will not be judged; do not condemn and you will not be condemned.'

If people really love one another and consider themselves a family, the Christian thing to do is to accept them as they describe themselves without condemnation.

The family is rapidly becoming the only institution in an increasingly impersonal world, where each person is loved not for what he or she does, but simply because he or she belongs and is God's unique creation. Can humanity survive destruction of the family?

Now prayerfully receive God's word on this important social and religious reality.

Family

It is from me that your family and every family in heaven and on earth takes its name.   *ref: Eph 3:14-15*

Your family ancestors have handed you on a faith that you may imitate them with sincerity . *ref: 2 Tim 1:4*

Husbands, love your wives as Christ loved his church and as you care for your own body. Never treat them harshly. *ref: Eph 5:25-33 and Col 3:19*

Wives, love and respect your husband as the church loves Christ.   *ref: Eph 5:22-24, 33*

It is my will that you be subject to one another out of reverence for my Son.   *ref: Eph 5:21*

Learn to discipline your children with love. It leads to peace, and they will respect you.   *ref: Heb 12:9-11*

Young women, love your husbands and your children. Be self-controlled, chaste and home builders.   *ref: Tit 2:4-5*

Young men, be self-controlled, be models of good works, of integrity and gravity. Be sound in speech that cannot be censured.   *ref: Tit 2:6-8*

Children, obey your parents in everything. This is your acceptable duty in the Lord.   *ref: Col 3:20*

Learn to provide for each other. This is your duty in faith. *ref: 1 Tim 5:8*

Old Testament culture was patriarchal. The father was the dominant member of the family. He had primacy in matters of property, discipline and in responsibility for the well being of the family. His major responsibility however was to communicate a living faith to his wife and children.

The Aramaic word *abba* was a familiar term for father. In the Old Testament it was almost never used for God. Of course no word can describe God. God is both father and mother and more. In our human efforts to know God, we are helped by comparing God to a father and a mother because God manifests the beautiful qualities which parents ideally manifest.

The New Testament uses the word *abba*, an intimate infant-sound, to express God's loving relationship with us. God is spoken of as father about two hundred and fifty times. This expresses the intimate relationship to which God invites us. When his apostles asked Jesus to teach them to pray, he did not say, 'Pray like this, Almighty God who art in heaven.' Rather, he instructed them to say, 'Our Father who art in heaven.'

The use of the word *abba* for prayer to God in Romans, in Galatians, in First Peter and in the Lord's prayer confirms our privilege of invoking God as Father. This cry comes from the Spirit of adoption within the believer. The Spirit makes us children of and gives us intimate access to the Father. It marks the end of legalism and servanthood.

Now, listen with reverence as God speaks of what is the ideal for every father.

Fatherhood

I am the one Father from whom are all things come and for whom all people exist.   *ref: 1 Cor 8:6*

I am the one Lord, the one God and Father of all, who is above all. through all and in all.   *ref: Eph 4:5-6*

From me, every fatherhood in heaven and on earth takes its name.   *ref: Eph 3:14*

May fathers inspire their children to honour them so that their children never have reason them to speak evil of them.   *ref: Mt 15:4*

May their fathers urge and encourage them, plead with them that they lead good lives worthy of me.   *ref: 1 Thess 2:11-12*

Let them inspire their children to work hard, and never to make promises they will not keep.   *ref: Mt 21:28-31*

When children request forgiveness, let it always be a time of celebration together, as it was for the prodigal son.   *ref: Lk 15:11-24*

May fathers love their children through discipline, but never provoke them to resentment lest they lose heart.   *ref: Col 3:21*

When illness strikes children like Jairus, let fathers pray for confidently healing.   *ref: Lk 8:40-42, 49-56*

In times of danger, may they protect their family with courage and fatherly care.   *ref: Mt 2:19-23*

In the Old Testament, the Greek word *meter* was used for human motherhood. It was also used to personify the nation, to describe the city (*metropolis*) and at times for mother earth.

In the book of Proverbs we are told 'Hear your Father's instruction and do not reject your mother's teaching' and 'a wise child makes a glad father but the foolish despise their mothers.'

God is generally portrayed as a Father, but even in the book of Isaiah we hear about the other side of God – God's motherly qualities – 'Can a mother forget her nursing child or show no compassion for the child of her womb? Even though they may forget I will not forget you.' In the deepest sense, God's love is like a father's or mother's love, but no metaphor can adequately describe God or Divine love.

Jesus compared his love for his people in these motherly terms, 'Jerusalem, Jerusalem ... how often I have desired to gather your children together as a hen gathers her brood under her wings and you were not willing.' God's love is compared to those protective maternal wings.

Seeing the feminine aspect of God brings fullness and a balance to our spirituality. Mother is the word for God in the hearts of infants when they first meet God in their mother's love, even without understanding any words.

Now gently listen to God describe his maternal love for you, and hear what is the ideal for your attitude towards all mothers.

Motherhood

I desire to gather all people together as a mother-hen gathers her brood under her wings.   *ref: Lk 13:34*

I send my Spirit on all mothers as I did on Mary, overshadowing them with my power.   *ref: Lk 1:35*

Mothers and grandmothers are privileged to pass faith to their offspring as Lois and Eunice did for Timothy.   *ref: 2 Tim 1:5*

Pray that mothers remain faithful when the sword of suffering pierces their hearts just as it pierced the mother of my Son.   *ref: Lk 2:35*

I bless their generosity when they share the little they sometimes have, as the poor widow did in the temple.
ref: Lk 21:1-4

I listen to mothers' prayers as my Son did when he blessed their children.   *ref: Mk 10:13-16*

Walk with mothers in their time of loss, as my Son did with the widow in Naim. Heal their sadness with your compassion.   *ref: Lk 7:11-15*

May mothers temper their ambition for their children. My loving plan for their welfare is best.   *ref: Mt 20:20-23*

There are two Greek words used for body in the New Testament. In the first chapter of his gospel, John speaks of God taking a body – 'The Word became flesh and lived among us.' John used the Greek word *sarx* to mean flesh considered as frail and mortal, meaning the full experience of being human. All of our bodies are dignified by God having taken our flesh.

Paul uses another word for flesh – *soma*. He uses it to present the body as something which must be kept unde filed, holy. He calls us to live in such a way that we reflect the selfless living and dying of Jesus in our bodies, by lives of loving self denial. In his letter to the Philippian community he says that Christ is to be magnified in our bodies and that we praise God in our bodies which are temples of the Holy Spirit. For believers then, the body ideally is a member of Christ and part of his mission to love.

An heretical sect called Gnostics regarded the body negatively, as a prison of the soul, and this false idea persisted in some Christian writers.

St James reminded us that our bodies need adequate food and clothing, and Paul tells Timothy that he should take care of his body, helping it to heal by taking a little wine.

Negative feelings about our bodies can be changed, and our self-image enhanced by adequate rest, by exercise, by dressing well, by sensible eating, by dance or by Christian yoga.

Now prayerfully hear these words of Jesus about the dignity and destiny of your body.

My Body

In the beginning I was with God; I was God. I became flesh in a body like yours.   *ref: 1 Jn 1:1-14*

Your body is now my holy temple. My Spirit dwells in you.   *ref: 1 Cor 3:16-17*

Take care to eat, and to clothe your body adequately, and to help others who need these essentials.   *ref: Jas 2:15-17*

Give your body adequate relaxation, with a restful holiday when you need it.   *ref: Mk 6:31*

But do not be anxious about your life, what you will eat or what you will wear.   *ref: Lk 12:32*

Do not let sin dominate your mortal body or make it obey its passions.   *ref: Rom 6:12*

Often lift up your hands in prayer, without anger or argument.   *ref: 1 Tim 2:8*

Your citizenship is in heaven where I will transform your body into the glorious body of my Son.   *ref: Phil 3:20-21*

Most of us tend not to think about death unless it takes someone we love, or we become terminally ill ourselves. Yet, it is useful to think about death before our final illness. Recognising that one day we have to let go of something precious helps us to value it more. Knowing that we do not have earthly life forever helps us to appreciate it all the more and to live it to its full.

Our faith adds a deeper dimension to these thoughts. After death we will encounter and enjoy God directly and forever. We will enter God's eternal now. We will be like God and see God in glory. We will be embraced by the infinite love which we sometimes doubted here below. By accepting love and giving love on earth, our hearts are being made ready to give love and to receive infinite love after death and forever. Teilhard de Chardin prayed, 'Teach me Lord, to treat my death as an act of communion.' Death ratifies the choice of God which we made every time we loved others on earth.

St Augustine assures us that after death we shall enjoy the company of our friends. And helping us to see the positive reality of death, Martin Luther said 'The Lord has written the promise of resurrection, not in scripture alone but in every leaf in springtime.' As we falteringly grow in faith, we gradually appreciate the words of Paul to his friends in Philippi, 'For to me living is Christ and dying is gain.'

Now listen deeply to God's words to you about your own death.

Death

Know that when your earthly tent is folded up, I have prepared for you a house not made with human hands, eternal
in the heavens.   *ref: 2 Cor 4:1*

I have given you a new birth into a living hope, into an
imperishable, undefiled and unfading inheritance through
the resurrection of my Son from the dead.   *ref: 1 Pet 3:4*

Do not lose heart then in old age when your outer nature
is wasting away. Your inner nature is being renewed day by
day.   *ref: 2 Cor 4:16*

What is sown is perishable. What will rise is immortal.
Death will be swallowed up in victory.   *ref: 1 Cor 15:42, 54*

Fight the good fight, finish the race and keep the faith.
Then I will give you the crown of righteousness because
you have longed for my appearing.   *ref: 2 Tim 4:7-8*

May you end your journey with the words of my Son, 'It is
fulfilled' and 'Into your hands I commend my spirit.'
ref Jn 19:30; Lk 23:46

Your friends need not grieve as those who have no hope. You
believed that my Son died and rose again. They know that I
will bring you and them with him one day.   *ref: Thess 4:13-14*

In most of the Old Testament there is only a vague mention of the individual's life after death. The Sadducees and the Samaritans did not believe in any resurrection.

But in his letter to the Roman Christians, Paul assures us, 'If the Spirit of him who raised Jesus from the dead dwells in you, he who raised Christ from the dead will give life to your mortal bodies also, through his Spirit that dwells in you.' Paul's deepest desire expressed to the Philippians was 'to know Christ and the power of his resurrection and the sharing of his sufferings by becoming like him in his death, if somehow I may attain the resurrection from the dead.' This desire can be ours.

In his first letter John tells us, 'Beloved, we are God's children now; what we will be has not yet been revealed. We shall be like him, for we shall see him as he is.'

The author of Ephesians sees our resurrection as having already taken place: 'God who is rich in mercy, out of the great love with which he loved us ... made us alive together with Christ ... and raised us up with him and seated us with him in the heavenly places in Christ Jesus'. We have only to accept this by living like Christ and with Christ in this world.

A Buddhist Master was asked by a pupil, 'Is there life after death?' The Master said, 'Do you hope so?' 'Yes,' the pupil replied. Then the then asked him, 'Where do think your hope come from?'

Now, reflect prayerfully on your own resurrection in Christ.

Resurrection

If for this life only you have hoped in my Son, you would be of all people most to be pitied.   *ref: 1 Cor 15:17-19*

But you were buried with him by baptism unto death. He was raised from the dead by my glory so that you can walk in newness of life.   *ref: Rom 6:4*

Continue to grow in your knowledge of him, and in the power of his resurrection. By sharing his sufferings, becoming like him in his death, you attain the resurrection from the dead.   *ref: Phil 3:8-11*

Live united with him in dying to yourself. You will certainly be united to him in his resurrection.   *ref: Rom 6:5*

By faith you are already alive together with Christ, already raised up with him, and seated with him in the heavenly places.   *ref: Eph 2:4-6*

My Son is the first fruits of those who have died. You will be made fully alive in him one day because you belong to him.   *ref: 1 Cor 15:20-23*

And because you have done good things here below, you will finally hear my voice calling you to the resurrection of life one day.   *ref: Jn 5:28-29*

WEEK FOUR

The church has always venerated the divine scriptures just as she venerates the body of the Lord, since, especially in the sacred liturgy, she unceasingly receives and offers the faithful the bread of life from the table both of God's word and of Christ's body'

Vatican II, *Word of God*, 21

In classical Greek the word for spirit was *pneuma*, meaning the wind or breath or life. It was also used to describe the spirit of joy among people or the spirit of a country. Because *pneuma* was deep, not controllable or predictable, the Greeks associated it vaguely with their gods, but not in any personal sense.

In the Old Testament the Hebrew word for spirit was *ruah*. It was also another word for breath, for the wind and for the life principle. Authors spoke of spirit as the centre of emotions, for example the spirit of joy or sadness, of courage or freedom and even of a desire for God. Genesis describes how God's breath or spirit in the form of a wind, blew before the creation of the world. The divine spirit was later given by the laying on of hands as when Moses laid his hands on Joshua.

In the New Testament the Spirit of God is revealed as a person. During his Last Supper, Jesus alarmed his disciples by saying that he was leaving them so that a deeper experience than his physical presence would come to them. 'It is to your advantage that I go away,' he said. He continued, 'For if I do not go away, the Advocate will not come to you, but if I go, I will send him to you.' This advocate, the Holy Spirit, the Spirit of love, was central to the life of Jesus and is central to our lives now.

Before you listen to God's word, ask the Holy Spirit to help you hear about his role in Jesus' life and in yours.

The Holy Spirit

My Holy Spirit came upon Mary, and my power overshadowed her so that her Son would be called my Son.
ref: Lk 1:35

I filled my Son with my Spirit before his birth so that he would be great in my sight.   *ref: Lk 1:15*

In the presence of the Spirit at the Jordan I identified my beloved Son in whom I am well pleased.   *ref: Mk 1:9-11*

The Spirit then led my Son into the desert to be tempted by the devil.   *ref: Mt 4:1*

Sent by my Son, the Holy Spirit testifies to him and enables you to testify to him also.   *ref: Jn 16:26-27*

By this you know my Spirit when you confess that my Son has come from me in the flesh.   *ref: 1 Jn 4:2*

You are not in the flesh, but in the Spirit. Since my Spirit dwells in you, you belong to Christ; he is in you.   *ref: Rom 8:9-10*

When you pray 'Abba, Father', my Holy Spirit bears witness with your spirit that you are my child, my heir and a joint heir with my Son.   *ref: Rom 8:15-17*

Until relatively recently, Western Christians paid inadequate attention to the Holy Spirit. Of course in the Acts of the Apostles there were baptised people who could say, 'We did not even know that there is a Holy Spirit.' And we read of those first Christians who 'were all astonished that the gift of the Holy Spirit should be poured out on the pagans too'. The Holy Spirit did not follow their narrow expectations.

With great care, and in very limited human language, we can say that the Holy Spirit is the love of the Father and the Son for each other in a person.

Experiencing God's love and then passing this love to others, is a sure manifestation of the Holy Spirit. The author of Ephesians tells us that another great measure of how we have accepted the Spirit of love is our willingness to proclaim God's message to others. And we are reminded that the opposites of love, such as falsehood, anger, stealing and evil talk, grieve the Holy Spirit with whose seal we are marked. He also reminds us that the Spirit wants us to take care in using only words that lovingly give grace and build others up. We love people most when we invite them to experience the fullness of God's love.

The Holy Spirit is not only someone to be prayed to but a life of love to be lived. In Galatians, Paul advises us to 'live by the Spirit' and to 'be guided by the Spirit'.

Now listen carefully to God speaking to you about living this new life, given to you and sustained in you by the Holy Spirit.

The Spirit of Love

As I promised through the prophets, I am pouring out my Spirit upon all flesh. *ref: Acts 2:17*

This Holy Spirit poured my love into your heart at your baptism. *ref: Rom 5:5*

If you love others, I abide in you and you abide in me, because I have given you my Spirit. *ref: 1 Jn 4:12-13*

If you are reviled for the name of my Son, you are blessed because the spirit of glory, my Spirit, is resting on you. *ref: 1 Pet 4:14*

My Spirit speaks through you when you proclaim my message, even in the face of opposition. *ref: Mt 10:19-20*

Speak only what is useful for building up. Let no evil talk come out of your mouth to grieve the Holy Spirit. Always be sure that your words are giving grace to those who hear you. *ref: Eph 4:29*

Hold to the sound teaching you have received with the help of the Holy Spirit living in you. Guard this good treasure entrusted to you. *ref: 2 Tim 1:13*

I have given you my Spirit as a guarantee that your mortality will one day be swallowed up in life. *ref: 2 Cor 5:4-5*

In the Old Testament, the Hebrew word *YHWH* is used for God. In the New Testament, the Greek translation of this word is *kyrios*. In our English Bible this word becomes Lord. Jesus is also called Lord, and likewise the Holy Spirit is Lord. In second Corinthians we read that 'The Lord is the Spirit.' Thus the divine name is used of all three persons.

Yet a different activity is ascribed to each member of the Trinity. The notion of power is attributed to the Holy Spirit, as when Mary is told that the power of the Most High will overshadow her. Similarly in Luke, Jesus told the apostles not to begin their ministry until they were clothed with power from the Holy Spirit, whom he promised to send them.

Paul spoke about a variety of gifts for service in the church but always from the same Spirit. There are apostles and prophets, evangelists and pastors, teachers, healers and others. He says that when each one is working well, it builds up the church in love. He asked his listeners to be eager for spiritual gifts.

Then there are gifts that are essential to every Christian life, the first one being love, then guidance, enrichment of our spiritual poverty, freedom from the captivity of sin and clarity for our spiritual blindness. As Jesus began his ministry in the synagogue, he tells us that these gifts come from the Holy Spirit. In his letter to the Galatians, Paul speaks of the fruit of the Spirit in its nine manifestations.

Now gently receive God's word to you about the gifts and the fruit of the Holy Spirit in your life.

Gifts and Fruit of the Spirit

My Spirit anointed Jesus to bring good news for your poverty, your captivity, your blindness and your oppression. *ref: Lk 4:8*

As a father gives good gifts to his children, so I also give the Holy Spirit to all who ask me.   *ref: Lk 11:13*

Do not grieve my Holy Spirit with which you were marked with a seal for the day of redemption.   *ref: Eph 4:30*

The fruit of my Spirit is love, joy, peace, patience, kindness, generosity, faithfulness, gentleness and self-control. *ref: Gal 5:22-23*

You will be guided towards your meeting with me when like Simeon you listen to my Spirit.   *ref: Lk 2:27*

My Holy Spirit can transform you into my image from one degree of glory to another.   *ref: 2 Cor 3:17-18*

As my Spirit enters your life, you receive power to be my witness before others.   *ref: Acts 1:8*

Through my Spirit who searches my depths, I reveal to you what no eye has seen, no ear has heard and no heart conceived what I have prepared for you who love me.   *ref: 1 Cor 2:9-10*

Our image of God is sometimes one of a God who is untouched by, or who perhaps does not really care about the emotional ups and downs, which are part of our human experience. However, John tells us that God became human, became flesh – *sarx* – a Greek word meaning human nature considered as weak and mortal.

In the letter to the Hebrews, we read that, because God in Christ did not come to help angels but weak human beings, he had to become 'like us his brothers and sisters in every respect'. He became 'subject to weakness', and able 'to sympathise with our weaknesses' because 'in every respect he was tested as we are, yet without sin'.

That weakness was particularly evident in the garden of Gethsemene where he was depressed, afraid, lonely, disappointed, unable to stand, anguished, weak and struggling to trust his Father. Describing his weakness, Luke tells us, 'In his anguish he prayed more earnestly, and his sweat became like great drops of blood falling down on the ground.'

The only power which God maintained and exercised in Jesus was the power of powerless loving. He relied on the power of love 'even to death on a cross'. However, despite his crucifixion, evil was not victorious because God vindicated him by raising him from the dead.

In Hebrews, we are encouraged, 'Let us therefore approach the throne of grace with boldness, so that we may receive mercy and find grace to help in time of need.'

Now prayerfully hear Jesus speak to you about his journey through human weakness by the power of God.

The Weakness of Christ

I was born in human likeness and found in human form.
ref: Phil 2:7

I was subject to weakness. I was tested in every way as you are, and so I deal gently with your waywardness. *ref: Heb 4:15; 5:2*

I became like you in every respect and was tested by what I suffered. *ref: Heb 2:17-18*

I felt tiredness as I sat by the well, and thirsty in the heat of the day. I knew hunger in the desert. *ref: Jn 4:6-10 and Mt 4:2*

I shared meals with sinners who were weak. *ref: Lk 5:29*

Grief and agitation filled my soul in the garden of Gethsemane. I was lonely and I asked for company. *ref: Mt 26:37-38*

I felt distressed, agitated and grieved even to death. I asked to escape the suffering of Calvary. *ref: Mk 14:33-36*

I felt the weakness of doubt about my Father's presence with me before my death on the cross. *ref: Mt 26:46*

I am able to sympathise with your weakness, and to give you mercy and grace in your time of need. *ref: Heb 4:16*

We obey freely when a request comes from someone we trust and it is beneficial to us or to others. Any other obedience would make us unwilling servants, not obeying from the heart.

The obedience of Jesus came freely from his heart. His Father was not an angry ruler demanding that his Son pay the price for our sins. Jesus knew that his suffering came from those who opposed his mission of love. Our salvation did not come because of Jesus' suffering, but in spite of this suffering. God was not punishing his Son for our sins nor sending him to die. He sent him rather to live and to love. The cross was the seal and culmination of his loving obedience to the Father.

He carried out his mission freely. He said, 'I lay down my life in order to take it up again. No one takes it from me, but I lay it down of my own accord.' His obedience was trusting, free and loving. He made this clear before leaving the supper room on his way to Gethsemene: 'I do as the Father has commanded me, so that the world may know that I love the Father. Rise, let us be on our way.'

Theologian Gerald O'Collins writes: 'Jesus' fidelity to his mission for God's kingdom inevitably brought him into conflict with the powerful political and religious people of his day. In such a conflict he was – humanly speaking – bound to lose. Loving service of those in need can turn people into targets. Both Christ and his heavenly Father willed the crucifixion indirectly – by accepting it.'

Now, listen prayerfully to the motivation for and the meaning of Christ's obedience to his mission.

The Obedience of Christ

My Father took no pleasure in burnt offerings but he gave me a body, and I said, 'Here I am coming to do your will' *ref: Heb 10:5-7*

He sent me to complete his work and my food was to do his will. *ref: Jn 4:34*

I did not cling to my equality with God but emptied myself into human form and became obedient to my Father unto death on a cross. *ref: Phil 2:6-8*

His loving will was that all who see me and believe in me would have eternal life. *ref: Jn 6:40*

It was his caring will that you be sanctified through the offering of my body. *ref: Heb 10:10*

The Father was with me always because I did what pleased him. *ref: Jn 8:29*

When my human feelings revolted, I prayed, 'Not my will but yours be done.' *ref: Lk 22:42*

Despite a deep feeling of having been forsaken, my last words to my Father were, 'It is fulfilled.' Then I bowed my head and gave up my spirit. *ref: Jn 19-30*

I glorified my Father on earth by finishing the work he gave me to do. *ref: Jn 17:4*

Our belief in the resurrection of Jesus is central to our Christian lives. Jesus predicted his own resurrection, but even after it took place, his followers found it difficult to believe. Mary of Magdala was the first to whom Jesus appeared, but she thought that he was the gardener. Peter and John doubted her when she said, 'I have seen the Lord.' Later they were astonished to find the empty tomb. Thomas in particular said he would not believe until he had put his finger into the holes in Jesus' hands. No wonder that Jesus said to the two disciples during a meal at Emmaus, 'You foolish men! So slow to believe all that the prophets have said.'

God acknowledged Jesus' life of trusting love and glorified him by raising him to life again. Ever since, Christians have made Christ's resurrection central to their faith and to their lives. We remember it, share it and celebrate it.

Paul assures us, 'In fact Christ has been raised from the dead, the first fruits of those who have died.' Opening his first letter, Peter gives us the same assurance in the form of a beautiful prayer: 'Blessed be the God and Father of our Lord Jesus Christ! By his great mercy he has given us a new birth into a living hope through the resurrection of Jesus Christ from the dead, and into an inheritance that is imperishable, undefiled and unfading, kept in heaven for you.'

Now, prayerfully accept God's invitation to deepen your faith and your privileged involvement in his Son's resurrection.

The Resurrection of Christ

I love my Son who laid down his life freely in order to take it up again.   *ref: Jn 10:17-18*

Having freed him from death, I raised him up because he could not to be held in death's power.   *ref: Acts 2:24*

To Martha and to you now he says, 'I am the resurrection and the life.'   *ref: Jn 11:25*

If my Son has not risen from the dead then your faith is in vain.   *ref: 1 Cor 15:14*

The angel assured Mary in her mourning, 'Do not be afraid. He is risen as he said.'   *ref: Mt 28:5-6*

At the empty tomb, he said to her, 'I ascend to my Father and to your Father.'   *ref: Jn 20:17*

After his resurrection, my Son's first greeting to his apostles was 'Peace be with you.'   *ref: Lk 24:36*

He is now head of the body, the church, the beginning, the first born from the dead.   *ref: Col 1:18-19*

One day, with all believers, you will be made alive in Christ. He is the first fruits, and then at his coming, you who belong to him will follow.   *ref: 1 Cor 15:23*

In the New Testament, the word *koinonia*, translated fellowship, is used principally to express our privilege of sharing the life of God together through Christ. In his first epistle, John stresses the joy of fellowship with the Father and the Son, a privilege he wishes to share with others. In Romans, Paul says that believers have fellowship in God's own divine nature as a branch which is grafted to a tree. Jesus said at the Last Supper, 'I am the vine, you are the branches.'

Our fellowship with God in Christ is a fact even now, although we await its full expression in heaven. Fellowship with Christ involves living like him, sharing in his suffering and death as we live out his gospel in our daily lives. This fellowship will lead one day to sharing the fullness of Christ's resurrection.

It also implies fellowship with other believers in shared faith, in love and in mutual service. The second chapter of the Acts of the Apostles gives us a beautiful description of the church in Christian fellowship through teaching, faith, Eucharist and prayer.

Taking part – *koinonia* – in the Lord's Supper is the pinnacle point of our fellowship with God and with others in Christ. In his first letter to the Christians of Corinth, Paul stresses that a shared Eucharist means a sharing of lives: 'As there is one loaf, so we, although there are many of us, are one single body, for we all share in the one loaf.'

Now, listen prayerfully to God's invitation to ever deeper fellowship with himself and with your fellow believers.

Fellowship with God

I am a faithful God who has called you into fellowship with my Son Jesus Christ your Lord. I will strengthen you to the end.   *ref: 1 Cor 1:8-9*

Your fellowship is with me and with my Son Jesus Christ. This must make your joy complete.   *ref: 1 Jn 1:3-4*

In this fellowship you are enabled to walk in the light and in the truth, not in lawlessness, darkness and lies.   *ref: 1 Jn 1:6-7; 2 Cor 6:14*

Your fellowship with me and my Son overflows into your fellowship with all believers.   *ref: 1 Jn 1:3-4*

As you walk in that light, you have fellowship with others and the blood of Jesus my Son cleanses you from all your sins.   *ref: 1 Jn 1:7*

By my divine power within you, you have all you need for life and godliness. To this way you are called as you share in my glory and goodness.   *ref: 2 Pet 1:3*

May the grace of your Lord Jesus Christ, my fatherly love and the fellowship of the Holy Spirit be with you and remain with you forever.   *ref: 2 Cor 13:13*

In the Old Testament, sacrifices usually called for the death of an animal. These were a recognition that all life, and especially one's own life, belonged to God. They were signs of one's total trust in and surrender to God. Without this sacrificial self-giving, external gestures were abominable in God's sight. In Psalms forty and fifty, praise, obedience, faithfulness and love are seen to be true sacrifices.

In Hebrews, Jesus says, 'Sacrifices and offering you have not desired, but a body you have prepared for me; in burnt offerings and in sin offerings you have taken no pleasure. Then I said, 'See, God, I have come to do your will, O God.'

Jesus set up a new covenant which found no place for cultic sacrifices. His life of total trust in God's love lived out in a life of love for others led to suffering and death. This was his sacrifice. He faithfully carried out his mission to mediate God's love to the world. The trusting faith underlying his life and his death was his sacrifice. We remember and celebrate the pinnacle point of this sacrificial life – his death – in the Eucharist.

Our faith and trust in God, expressed in self-giving love for others, is our sacrifice. It is united to the sacrificial life and death of Jesus, and it leads to a gradual death to ourselves and to living for God, which is resurrection. In the case of those killed for confessing their faith or in their struggle for justice, Jesus' sacrifice is particularly manifest. These men and women lived the Eucharist in a very complete way.

Now, God's word invites you to grow in sacrificial faith.

Sacrifice

Your deepest sacrifice and offering to me is your faith, your trust in me. Rejoice and be glad in that.   *ref: Phil 2:17-18*

As my beloved child, live your faith in love of others, just as my Son loved you when he gave himself up for you, a fragrant offering and sacrifice to me.   *ref: Eph 5:1-2*

You are precious in my sight. Come to me as a holy priesthood to offer spiritual sacrifices acceptable to me through my Son Jesus Christ.   *ref: 1 Pet 2:4-5*

Through him, continue to offer a sacrifice of praise to me, the fruit of your lips that confess his name.   *ref: Heb 13:15*

I appeal to you by my mercy to present your body as a living sacrifice, holy and acceptable to me which is your spiritual worship.   *ref: Rom 12:1*

Do not neglect to do good, to share what you have, for such sacrifices are pleasing to me.   *ref: Heb 13:16*

These gifts to the needy are fragrant offerings, acceptable sacrifices pleasing to me.   *ref: Phil 4:18*

My Son the paschal lamb has been sacrificed. Celebrate the festival, not with the old yeast but with the unleavened bread of sincerity and truth.   *ref: 1 Cor 5:7*

The word Eucharist means thanksgiving. People often cele brate their friendship and their gratitude for it at a meal together. Believers usually begin or end meals with prayers of thanksgiving. Meals are also an occasion to offer hospitality.

At his last meal with his apostles, Jesus ended it by say ing, 'Do this in memory of me.' This meal was followed by great suffering and his death. These events were foreshad owed in the celebration of the meal when Jesus said that in the bread and wine his body was given and his blood was shed for others. The meal expressed and enacted the sacrifi cial aspect of Christ's suffering and death. Christians continue to celebrate this sacrificial meal together, this expression of a new covenant, as Paul reminds us in First Corinthians.

Eucharist is a re-enactment and a ritual recognition that God loves us irrevocably in Christ and that we love one another. In the Eucharist we recognise that we are forgiven, nourished, healed and sanctified. For this we express grati tude.

The experience of eating bread together is linked to the word *companion* that comes from the Latin *cum-panis* which literally means 'with bread'. Only those who are true companions, in the sense that they love one another, can celebrate Eucharist together. It is usually preceded by a sharing and communion in the scriptures.

This sharing together in the body and blood of Christ has obvious social and political implications too. It calls believers to be companions to the underprivileged and the undernourished of the world.

Now listen in prayer as Jesus speaks to you about this sacrificial meal, the central act of our Christian liturgy.

Eucharist

Coming into the world, my sentiments were these – 'Sacrifice and offerings you have not desired, but a body you have prepared for me ... Then I said, 'See, I come to do your will, O God'.   *ref: Heb 10:5-7*

I bore your sins in my body on the cross so that free from sins you might live in righteousness. By my wounds you were healed.   *ref: 1 Pet 2:24*

At my last supper I took the loaf of bread, I broke it and gave it to my friends saying, 'This is my body which is given for you'.   *ref: Lk 22:19*

The bread that you now break, is it not a sharing in my body? Because there is one bread, you who are many are one body, for you all partake of the one bread.   *ref: 1 Cor 10:16-17*

As often as you eat this bread and drink this cup, you proclaim my death until I come.   *ref: 1 Cor 11:26*

Examine yourself before you eat of the bread and drink of the cup. For all who eat and drink without discerning my body, eat and drink judgement against themselves.   *ref: 1 Cor 11:27-29*

When you eat my flesh and drink my blood, you abide in me, and I in you. Just as the Father sent me and I live because of the Father, so whoever eats my body will live because of me.   *ref: Jn 6:56-57*

Obedience is often thought of as doing what a law commands. Even respected institutions can emphasise this.

Paul, once a Pharisee, had led a life of obedience to a rigid religious system. He said that he lived in bondage to a religion of law. After his conversion he said that Christ had set him free from all that, and he rejoiced in his new-found freedom. Law no longer motivated his moral life; it was his identity with and his love of Christ that inspired his obedience from then on.

The obedience of the baptised is not life under law. The law has been superceded by the gospel which Paul calls 'the law of Christ'. Christian obedience comes from within, not from an external law. The scripture scholar Wilfrid Harrington calls our obedience to the gospel 'the visible dynamic of being-in-Christ'.

Dependence on law could bring a false sense of security, an immaturity hampering love. Law can blunt our response to God if we limit our behaviour to what is prescribed.

Christian obedience is an act of faith put into practice. It is belief that our God is a wise God whose will is an expression of love, a divine wish for our welfare and for the welfare of others. God's will does not always lead to obvious or immediate success, but it is always for our good.

The call to Christian obedience demands profound listening with an open heart, usually with the help of other believers, to hear the voice of God who loves us and who knows what is best for us.

Now hear and receive God's liberating word on the real meaning of Christian obedience.

Obedience of Faith

My Son sent his church to make disciples of all nations, and to teach them to obey everything he commanded. He promised to be with his church to the end of the age. *ref: Mt 28:19-20*

From the church you received faith, and you were graced to hear my Son's message. ref: *Rom 1:4-6; 10:14-17*

Give thanks that when you received the word, you accepted it as my word, and that it is still at work in you as a believer. *ref: 1 Thess 2:13*

Always remain united in faith with those who listen, lest the benefits of my message fail to reach you. *ref: Heb 4:1-2*

By purifying your soul in obedience to the truth you will love others deeply from the heart. *ref: 1 Pet 1:22*

I have created you in my Son for good works, so that this may be your way of life. *ref: Eph 2:10*

My Son learned obedience through what he suffered, and having been made perfect he became the source of salvation for all who obey him. *ref: Heb 5:8-9*

You are blessed when you hear my word and obey it. *ref: Lk 11:28*

You have received grace and apostleship to bring others to the obedience of faith also. *ref: Rom 1:5*

In the Old Testament we read about religious people who were tempted to doubt God's love or God's presence in their lives.

Jesus was tempted in the desert. In Gethsemane he overcame another temptation to give up his mission. On the cross, Jesus struggled and prayed, 'My God, my God, why have you forsaken me?' At these times he simply surrendered to God's plan.

Most people have questions about how God acts in their lives. We all sometimes lack confidence in God's love, and even doubt God's existence. This happens usually at a time of suffering or crisis in our lives. But to have faith is to have doubts because faith is a journey; we are all growing in faith.

To the Corinthians, Paul wrote: 'God is faithful and he will not let you be tested beyond your strength, but with the testing he will also provide the way out so that you may be able to endure it.'

Our failures also test our faith. Meister Eckhart wrote 'One seldom finds that people attain to anything good unless first they have gone somewhat astray.'

Karl Rahner encouragingly tells us: 'Christianity is not a religion that solves all the riddles of the universe. Faith in Christ gives one the courage to shelter oneself in an incomprehensible mystery and to believe that this mystery is love.'

The last line of the Our Father is better translated, 'Do not bring us to the test.'

Now, prayerfully accept God's encouraging words in your struggles with faith and doubt in your life.

Testing of Faith

My Son was put to the test in exactly the same way as you are, enabling him to help you when you are tested.   *ref: Heb 2:18; 4:15*

He was tempted to indulgence, to pride, to power. He used my word to drive the devil away.   *ref: Mt 4:1-11*

Approach his throne of grace boldly, to receive mercy and help in time of need.   *ref: Heb 4:16*

When my word is deeply rooted in your heart, you will not fall away in time of testing.   *ref: Lk 8:13*

I am faithful and you will not be tested beyond your strength.   *ref: 1 Cor 10:13*

When you are tempted, it is not I who tempt you. You are tempted by your own desire.   *ref: Jas 1:14*

When you face trials of any kind, it is a joy because the testing of your faith brings endurance, maturity, completeness.   *ref: Jas 1:2-4*

Rejoice if for a little while you have various trials so that the genuineness of your faith is tested. Your victory will result in praise, glory and honour when my Son is revealed.   *ref: 1 Pet 1:6-7*

Our God is three divine persons, and each of them shares completely with the other in everything. As John puts it so simply, 'God is love'. It is not just that God loves; God is identified with love. The very nature of God is to love, to share friendship. The pagan gods shared only when they were praised or as a reward for expected behaviour.

In limited human language, the true God can be described as Infinite Freedom for Infinite Love, as infinite freedom expressing itself in infinite self-giving, in unlimited sharing. We are finite freedoms for love, made in God's image and likeness. We are made to reflect God's infinite freedom for love. By our very nature we are made and called to love, to share.

John reminds us, 'Those who abide in love, abide in God.' To abide in God is to love others, to share. Those who do not abide in love, do not abide in God.

The greatest thing we can share is our faith, our friendship with God. When we 'abide in God' we cannot but desire to share God with others. And of course, what is worth having is worth sharing.

Our God is a sharing God. If God ceased sharing the divine friendship, God would no longer be God. In John's gospel, Jesus tells us that God sent him to share the divine life: 'I have come that they may have life and have it abundantly'. We are sent in a similar way, that others may have a share in the divine life, in the divine friendship, through faith.

Now, prayerfully hear God inviting you to appreciate and to share the greatest gift you possess.

Sharing of Faith

My Son prayed that believers would share our oneness, to be one with us, just as we are one.   *ref: Jn 17:20-23*

All people are invited to become fellow heirs with my Son, members of the same body and sharers in the promise through the gospel.   *ref: Eph 3:6*

So that you may share in my holiness, I discipline you for your good. This discipline will yield the peaceful fruit of righteousness.   *ref: Heb 12:10-11*

May the sharing of your faith with others become effective when you perceive all the good you may do for my Son.   *ref: Philem 6*

Meet your friends to share some spiritual gifts with them and to strengthen one another in faith.   *ref: Rom 1:11*

Share the weakness of others for the sake of the gospel, so that you may share in its blessings.   *ref: 1 Cor 9:23*

I appeal to you to contend for the faith as you eagerly share the gift of salvation with others.   *ref: Jude 1:3*

Jesus assured us that if we continue in his word, we will know the truth and that this truth will set us free. In his human nature, he made God's word his life and that truth set him free. His total trust in God, his life lived for others, and finally his death, were expressions of his faith and of this freedom. He was free enough to become the perfect image and real symbol of God's presence in the world. The belief that he was loved by his Father was the source of his freedom.

Karl Rahner tells us that being free is faith. He says that faith is not an act that is free, as though freedom were a result of faith. Faith is the fullest expression of freedom. Lived faith is being free, and it is a gift from God. Our faith lived out is the measure of how free we are. It is freedom from selfishness and from sin in order to be free for love.

Jesus himself reminds us that sin is slavery and Paul reminded the Galatians that Christ has set us free. Freedom from uncontrolled surrender to selfish instincts which seek power, status or wealth, is faith in action. Our deepest freedom, given by the Holy Spirit of love, as it was in Jesus, is firstly the freedom to believe that we are loved unconditionally by God. It is the same freedom that enables us to love others as God loves us. Only in freedom can we direct ourselves towards goodness, towards God.

The church teaches that salvation is 'a precious gift which is freedom from anything that oppresses the human person, especially freedom from sin and the evil one'.

Now gratefully hear God invite you to the fullness of freedom.

Freedom

Where my Spirit is there is freedom, as I transform you into my glorious image.   *ref: 2 Cor 17:18*

By your baptism I have freed you from sin and death. I invite you to walk in this newness of life.   *ref: Rom 6:1-7*

Everyone who commits sin is a slave to sin. How can you who died to sin in your baptism go on living in it? *ref: Jn 8:34; Rom 6:2*

For freedom my Son has set you free. Stand firm then and do not submit to a yoke of slavery called sin.   *ref: Gal 5:1*

If you continue in my word you are truly my disciple. You will know the truth that will make you free.   *ref: Jn 8:31-32*

I invite you to live as a free person in loving and in serving one another.   *ref: Gal 5:13*

Never use your freedom as an opportunity for evil. *ref: 1 Pet 2:16; Gal 5:13-14*

One day, all creation will be free from its bondage to decay, to obtain the freedom of the glory of my children.   *ref: Rom 8:19-21*

To my Son who loves you and who freed you from your sins by his blood, may there be glory and dominion forever and ever. Amen.   *ref: Rev 1:5-6*

To have peace in one's heart is the deepest need of the human person. People who are ill or materially poor sometimes have peace when healthy or wealthy people lack it.

In the Old Testament, the Hebrew word *shalom* for peace denoted a sense of total well-being. God made a Covenant with the people and this resulted in wellbeing or *shalom*. It was God's gift to the people and finally it came to denote a relationship between themselves. Yet, in the Old Testament *shalom* generally stressed security. Only gradually did it come to mean moral goodness.

In the New Testament, the Greek word for peace is *eirene*. It came to mean an inner harmony; it was first used in greetings. Jesus' first words to his apostles after his resurrection were 'Peace be with you.' Paul greets his friend Timothy with the words, 'Grace and peace' and Peter ends his first letter, 'Peace to you all who are in Christ.' In his second letter, Peter equates peace with perfect wellbeing which is being God-like. Writing to the Romans Paul calls God the God of peace.

Christian peace embraces the salvation of the whole person. When the Roman Christians were quarrelling, Paul exhorted them to pursue what made for peace among them. The author of Ephesians says that Christ is our peace and he ends his letter with these words, 'Peace be to the whole community, and love with faith from God our Father and the Lord Jesus Christ.'

Now prayerfully hear and accept the full meaning of God's gift of peace in your heart.

Peace of Heart

At the birth of my Son, the angels announced peace.   *ref:*
Lk 2:14

He is the world's peace. He has given all groups the power
to be united in peace.   *ref: Eph 2:14*

My desire is one reconciled humanity, living in peace.   *ref:*
Eph 2:15-16

A peace the world cannot give was my Son's last gift to
you. Do not let your heart be troubled or afraid.   *ref: Jn 14:27*

I, the God of hope, wish to fill you with all joy and peace
in your believing.   *ref: Rom 15:13*

Even in the face of difficult decisions, it is to peace that I
call you.   *ref: 1 Cor 7:15*

You are blessed when you are a peacemaker; you will be
called my child.   *ref: Mt 5:9*

I invite you to pursue what makes for peace and for the
building up of others.   *ref: Rom 14:19*

May mercy, peace and love always be yours in abundance.
ref: Jude 3

Speaking to God, the Psalmist wrote: 'In your presence there is fullness of joy; at your right hand are pleasures forever.' The believer's relationship with God was a source of joy, and it enabled the Psalmist to write also: 'The laws of the Lord are right, rejoicing the heart.' After God's loving care and guidance, the people of the Old Testament found a constant source of joy in recalling and celebrating God's saving acts from the past. It is in recalling these and in trust for the future, that the faith-filled person finds a deep inner spring of joy.

Luke makes frequent mention of joy, for instance at the coming of the Saviour, at the lost being found, and at the thought of one's name being written in heaven. In Jesus' final discourse he told us that he loves us as the Father loves him, and he revealed this to us so that his joy would be ours. This joy is not just a shallow feeling of excitement; it is a much deeper and permanent state, even in the presence of pain and suffering.

At a moment when sadness might be expected, we read in the last line of Luke's gospel that the apostles returned from the Mount of the Ascension to Jerusalem 'with great joy'. Later, even after the apostles had been flogged they rejoiced, not in their suffering, but at having suffered for Christ. In his first letter, John said that he was telling others about Jesus in order to increase his own joy.

Now confidently believe that as you listen, these words of God will increase divine joy in you.

Joy

As your God, I offer you good news and great joy. My Son your Saviour has come. Never be afraid. *ref: Lk 2:10*

I offer you my word , inviting you to rejoice in me, God your Saviour. *ref: Lk 1:46-47*

Rejoice in my Spirit. My mysteries have been revealed to you and your name is written in heaven. *ref: Lk 10:20-31*

Rejoice then in me always; again I say rejoice. *ref: Phil 4:4*

You have not seen me but you believe in me, and a joy indescribable and glorious is already yours. *ref: 1 Pet 1:8*

Rising above difficulties and inspired by the Holy Spirit, continue to receive my word with joy. *ref: 1 Thess 1:6*

You may have pain now, but no one can take my joy from you. *ref: Jn 16:22*

The fruit of my Spirit is love, joy and peace. When you live by my Spirit, you will be guided by him. *ref: Gal 5:22, 25*

My kingdom is not food and drink, but righteousness, peace and joy brought by the Holy Spirit. *ref: Rom 14:17*

Because you have loved others with the love I gave you, you will enter into my own joy one day. *ref: Mt 25:21*

In the letter to the Ephesians we read that each of us is 'God's work of art'. Every person is a manifestation of God. In Psalm 139 we read, God 'knit me together in my mother's womb'. Each of us is a once-for-all knitting together by God.

We each manifest God's glory in a unique and irreplaceable way. Each one's personality and spirituality – the way we meet God – is unique too. A person's experience of God is always influenced by one's genetic endowment, one's developmental history, one's culture, race, social class and of course by one's sexuality.

Men and women experience and manifest God differently. Since all language about God is metaphorical, not literal, every image of God is incomplete. Maleness has no priority in imaging God. Language drawn from women's experience of themselves and of God is as appropriate as male language in helping us meet God.

For cultural reasons, the Bible and the church have in the past emphasised the male image of God. This has led to a narrow, one-sided and undernourished spirituality. Men now need to meet the God-experience of women.

Speaking in Antwerp in 1985, Pope John Paul II said: 'The faithful community expects the enriching intervention of women, not only in the family, but in theological thinking, in the life of the community, in missionary vocations, in consultative bodies and in pastoral ministries.'

Now prayerfully reflect on these encounters of Jesus with women.

Woman

My chosen place for relaxation was at Bethany in the home of my beloved Martha, Mary and their brother Lazarus. *ref: Lk 10:38*

I publically forgave a woman condemned by leaders, and asked her not to sin again.   *ref: Jn 8:1-11*

I condemned those men who would treat women as sexual objects even in their desires.   *ref: Mt 5:28*

I compared a woman's joy at finding lost coins with the joy of my Father when you repent.   *ref: Lk 15:8-10*

On my way to heal a little girl at her mother's request, I rewarded the faith and the humility of a woman who touched my garment.   *ref: Mk 5:30*

At Simon's house, I appreciated the woman's generous public anointing of my body in preparation for my burial. *ref: Mt 26:6-13*

When the scholarly men of Athens scoffed at my resurrection, a woman named Damaris became one of the first believers.   *ref: Acts 17:32-33*

From my cross, I asked my mother to care for my beloved disciple and I asked him to care for her.   *ref: Jn 19:25-27*

It was to Magdalen that I first spoke after my resurrection. I chose her to bring the news to my frightened apostles. *ref: Jn 20:16-18*

In the time of Jesus women were repressed by society and by religious leaders. Jesus would have been familiar with the warning of some rabbis, 'It is better to give the Torah to a dog than to a woman', and with the prayer, 'I thank thee Yahweh that you have not made me a dog, a Samaritan or a woman.' A rabbi was forbidden to speak to a woman in public. Jesus challenged these laws publically and as a result he liberated women in many ways.

Women were said to have destroyed harmony in the garden of Eden, and girls were taught to be subordinate because Eve was created to help Adam. These attitudes permeated Old Testament times and remained for hundreds of years later. This was despite the New Testament teaching that women and men are equally baptised into Christ and that in Christ there is neither male nor female. Of course, the unique and canonised holiness of women, many of whom were martyrs, was always recognised in the church. Most of us have known and been profoundly inspired by holy women, especially our mothers.

In *Mulieris Dignitatem*, Pope John Paul II wrote: 'The moment is coming when woman's vocation will be fully realised; the moment when woman takes on in the world an influence, a radiance, a power until now unattained. That is why at this time, when humanity is undergoing so many changes, women filled with the spirit of God can do so much to help humanity not to fail.'

Now prayerfully hear Jesus speak to you about women in his life.

Woman

When the fullness of God's time had come, I was born of a woman so that you might receive adoption as God's child.   *ref: Gal 4:4-5*

My mother Mary was the consenting cause of my incarnation.   *ref: Lk 1:38*

The old woman Anna praised God at my birth and spoke of me as the liberator of Jerusalem.   *ref: Lk 2:36-38*

I recognised the dignity of women when I spoke to them contrary to religious custom.   *ref: Jn 4:27*

I talked to Mary in Bethany about the importance of listening to my word.   *ref: Lk 10:42*

I publicly defended a woman who came to honour me during a meal with Simon the leper.   *ref: Mk 14:6*

I called attention to a generous widow as an example to my apostles.   *ref: Mk 12:41-44*

I rewarded the faith of a foreign woman by curing her distressed daughter.   *ref: Mt 15:21-28*

After accepting the graciousness of a sinful woman who wept at my feet, I showed how forgiveness leads to deeper love.   *ref: Lk 7:47*

When my apostles deserted me, it was faithful women who in the end, with John, took their stand beneath my cross. *ref: Jn 19:25*

Anglican theologian John Maquarrie reminds us that 'Mary was chosen as the last link in the chain before the appearance of Christ.' Mary herself said that, 'The Mighty One had done great things for me' and she predicted, 'all generations will call me blessed.'

In the past, Mary was seen as a passive instrument in the hands of God, but now she is considered to have played a more active role. Anglican theologian Pittenger calls her 'the consenting cause of the incarnation'.

Elizabeth said that Mary was first blessed in receiving Christ by faith, before conceiving him in her flesh – 'Blessed is she who believed that the word spoken to her would be fulfilled.' Mary is a model for believers. She heard God's word, she dialogued, she discerned and she decided to take the risk of faith, which for her could have led to desertion or to death by stoning.

Mary is now seen as encouraging the church's stance on the side of the poor. In the words of her *Magnificat*: 'He has brought down the powerful from their thrones, and lifted up the lowly.' Her presence at Calvary, and after that with the apostles in the Cenacle, also show her to have had an active role in the early church.

In his commentary on the *Magnificat*, Martin Luther wrote: 'O blessed Virgin Mary, how have you been considered as nothing, and distained as of little consequence, seeing that God has regarded you with all his grace, and accomplished such mighty things in you.'

Now like Mary, who received God's word, prayerfully accept Jesus' words for you.

Mary

Elizabeth reminds you that my mother Mary is a model for your faith in my Father's word . *ref: Lk 1:45*

May my Father's word become incarnate in you as it did in Mary, with openness, fruitfulness and joy.   *ref: Lk 1:38*

My mother shares in your times of loss and anxiety just as she was distressed when I was missing as a child.   *ref: Lk 2:41-50*

When trial and suffering come your way, recall that she too endured the sword of pain foretold by Simeon.   *ref: Lk 2:35*

At times of failure to understand my Father's ways, may you, like my mother, treasure God's words in your heart. *ref: Lk 2:50-51*

On your journey in faith, recall often her advice to the waiter at Cana, to do whatever I ask of you.   *ref: Jn 2:5*

After each encounter with God in prayer, may you move to help others like my mother did.   *ref: Lk 1:38-39*

May you stand alongside those rejected by society today, as my courageous mother took her stand beneath my cross. *ref: Jn 19:25*

As my mother was present with the first apostles, may she inspire all believing women to take their rightful place with church leaders today.   *ref: Acts 1:14*

Wisdom is a combination of clear thinking, open-mindedness, readiness to weigh alternatives and an attempt to see the big picture. It also implies a readiness to seek advice from wise friends, and of course it presupposes a readiness to change one's mind.

In the Old Testament, the Hebrew word-group for wisdom – *hakam* – occurs over three hundred times. The wise person was one who was sensitive to God and who applied God's guidance to life. In the book of Proverbs, wisdom becomes a person and the Greek noun used is feminine – *sophia*. There we are told that 'Wisdom does not enter a deceitful soul.'

The New Testament also uses the word *sophia* for wisdom. In his first letter to the Corinthian community, Paul tells us that 'the wisdom of this world is foolishness with God', and that it leads to disunity and divisions. Instead, he recommends that people get in touch with God's thoughts wherein lies true wisdom. Then he identifies wisdom with 'Christ Jesus who became for us wisdom from God' and he adds that this is the wisdom with which we must be filled.

In Ephesians we read that 'the wisdom of God in its rich variety' comes to us through the church. Paul tells the Colossians that when the word of Christ dwells in us richly we can 'admonish one another in all wisdom'. In the first chapter of the same letter he offers us a beautiful prayer for spiritual wisdom, so that we can 'lead lives worthy of the Lord and fully pleasing to him.'

Now, reflect prayerfully and deeply on God's word to you about wisdom.

Wisdom

The depths of my riches and of my wisdom are unsearchable.   *ref: Rom 11:33*

My wisdom can be learned only through the Spirit who interprets spiritual things for those who are spiritual.   *ref: 1 Cor 2:9-13*

I made foolish the wisdom of the world. My foolishness is wiser than human wisdom.   *ref: 1 Cor 1:20-25*

My Son Jesus is your wisdom, your righteousness, your sanctification and your redemption.   *ref: 1 Cor 1:30*

The message about his cross seems foolish, but my crucified Son is still my wisdom.   *ref: 1 Cor 1:17-25*

So that you may have knowledge of Christ, in whom are hidden all the treasures of wisdom, I want your heart to be encouraged by others and united with them in love.   *ref: Col 2:2-3*

Be aware that human commands and teaching that promote self-imposed piety, humility and severe treatment of your body have only an appearance of wisdom.   *ref: Col 2:22-23*

When you have true wisdom you will show it by your good works, always done with gentleness.   *ref: Jas 3:13*

In the Old Testament God asked the people to wait patiently for the divine actions. Sometimes they succeeded and sometimes they failed. Job is the great example of waiting even in the face of undeserved suffering. When we are suffering it is especially difficult to wait in faith for God's healing.

In the Acts of the Apostles, Luke reminds the first Christians that waiting in persecution may be necessary until Christ comes again. Writing to the Romans, Paul, who suffered from tiredness, discouragement, beatings, illness and old age, says that our patient suffering will not be disappointed.

John speaks about our abiding in Christ, who then enables us to wait confidently for his second coming. In Hebrews we are reminded that 'Christ will appear a second time, not to deal with sin, but to save those who are eagerly waiting for him.' And James assures us that our patient endurance helps us to become mature, complete and lacking in nothing. In Romans, Paul says that like us, the rest of creation waits for its full redemption. He considers the destiny of the created world to be linked with the future of believers.

After Jesus' Ascension, the apostles were keen to proclaim the good news, but he had told them to wait in Jerusalem for the coming of the Holy Spirit before beginning their mission. Our time is not always God's time.

A frequent prayer of Christians down through the centuries has been the second last verse in the New Testament 'Come, Lord Jesus'.

Now, prayerfully reflect on the wisdom of patient waiting for God's time in your life.

Patient Waiting

Follow the example of my devout servant Simeon. He rejoiced when his waiting was rewarded.   *ref: Lk 2:25-32*

All creation joins you as you await the redemption of your body. Wait then in patience for what you do not yet see. *ref: Rom 8:19-25*

Hold fast to my word with an honest and good heart, and bear fruit with patient endurance.   *ref: Lk 8:15*

Through the Spirit and by faith, wait eagerly for the hope of righteousness.   *ref: Gal 5:5*

You are not lacking in any spiritual gift, as you look forward to the revealing of our Lord Jesus Christ. He will strengthen you to the end so that you can be blameless when he comes.   *ref: 1 Cor 1:7-8*

Pray with expectant faith like my Son's apostles as they looked forward to the Spirit's coming.   *ref: Acts 1:4*

Live a life that is self-controlled, upright and godly as you wait for the manifestation of my glory.   *ref: Tit 2:12:13*

Remember I will come a second time to save those who eagerly await my coming.   *ref: Heb 9:28*

John tells us that Eternal Life is knowing God and Jesus Christ whom he has sent. Church work, theological study, Bible reading, social action and even prayer itself could be kinds of busyness that slow down or shut out a personal knowledge of God.

It is only by mutual loving that we truly know any friend well. We can know *about* another person – their external strengths and weaknesses, but until we approach the other in love and total trust, we cannot really know them. To know God as a friend then, is to take the risk that any deep relationship will involve – the risk of stepping into the unknown, into total trust of the other.

Until we are lovingly open to allowing the God of love to envelop us, we risk only knowing *about* God but never encountering the Divine Persons. We also risk reducing the richness of our Christian lives to serving God merely by obeying commandments. In Philippians, Paul tells us that knowledge of God is a gradual acceptance of the miracle that God has 'made me his own'.

Our relationship with God involves a trusting letting go of ourselves into God's welcoming arms. The Spirit of God will always need the space of an empty heart. We have to be empty of self to be filled with God. It is in this empty heart, in this sacred space, that we will meet the God of love who will bring us beyond our deepest imaginings. Graced self-surrender is the only path to the divine.

Now, hear God's loving word enabling you to grow in your relationship with the Divine.

Knowing God

I made the world and everything in it. I am Lord of heaven and earth.   *ref: Acts 17:24*

I am not a deity made of gold or silver or stone, an image formed by the imagination of mortals.   *ref: Acts 17:29*

Ever since the creation of the world, my eternal power and divine nature, invisible though they are,can be seen in the things I have created.   *ref: Rom 1:20*

Lofty words or human wisdom cannot lead you to the mystery of my being.   *ref: 1 Cor 2:1*

Pray for wisdom and revelation that the eyes of your heart may be enlightened as you come to know me.   *ref: Eph 1:17-18*

Pray for spiritual wisdom and understanding to grow in your knowledge of me.   *ref: Col 1:9-10*

Encouragement and love of one another will also give you knowledge and understanding of the mystery which is me.   *ref: Col 2:2*

Knowledge inflated with pride, but love builds up. Anyone who loves me knows me and is known by me.   *ref: 1 Cor 8:1-3*

Thematic Index